God's mercies are new every morning! We are to regard our body (the temple of the Lord) as a grateful presentation to Him every day. Dr. Davis blends her medical knowledge, practical experience, essential facts, and the Word of God to help us become our personal change agents for a healthy lifestyle. Having gone through a life-threatening illness myself, I know the value of following a plan like this to guide us to complete health. You can begin to improve your health TODAY by following the plan in this book!

—Thelma Wells, DD
President, A Woman of God Ministries
Speaker/author/mentor
www.thelmawells.com

Dr. Kara Davis has gone to the core of the issue and offers hope and dependable advice to the person who is ready to get serious about weight loss!

—Jan Silvious
Author, *Moving Beyond the Myths*
Conference speaker

With great sensitivity and spiritual insight, Dr. Kara Davis attacks the underlying causes of dangerous food obsessions. Her groundbreaking approach will bring health and deliverance because it doesn't treat symptoms; it exposes spiritual roots of our problems.

—Brenda Davis
Acquisitions editor, Strang Book Group
Former editor, *SpiritLed Woman* magazine

Dr. Davis addresses a major health problem in a godly, good, an... ... than just identify the p...

Henry M. Williamson Sr.
...ng Prelate, Ninth District
...thodist Episcopal Church

D1052891

Spiritual Secrets *to* Weight Loss

KARA DAVIS, MD

SILOAM
A STRANG COMPANY

Most STRANG COMMUNICATIONS BOOK GROUP products are available at special quantity discounts for bulk purchase for sales promotions, premiums, fund-raising, and educational needs. For details, write Strang Communications Book Group, 600 Rinehart Road, Lake Mary, Florida 32746, or telephone (407) 333-0600.

SPIRITUAL SECRETS TO WEIGHT LOSS by Kara Davis, MD
Published by Siloam: A Strang Company
600 Rinehart Road
Lake Mary, Florida 32746
www.strangbookgroup.com

Unless otherwise noted, all Scripture quotations are from the Holy Bible, New International Version. Copyright © 1973, 1978, 1984, International Bible Society. Used by permission.

Scripture quotations marked AMP are from the Amplified Bible. Old Testament copyright © 1965, 1987 by the Zondervan Corporation. The Amplified New Testament copyright © 1954, 1958, 1987 by the Lockman Foundation. Used by permission.

Scripture quotations marked KJV are from the King James Version of the Bible.

Scripture quotations marked NAS are from the New American Standard Bible. Copyright © 1960, 1962, 1963, 1968, 1971, 1972, 1973, 1975, 1977 by the Lockman Foundation. Used by permission. (www.Lockman.org).

Design Director: Bill Johnson; Cover design by Karen Grindley

Library of Congress Cataloging-in-Publication Data:
Davis, Kara.
  Spiritual secrets to weight loss / Kara Davis.
     p. cm.
  ISBN 978-1-59979-377-1
  1. Fruit of the Spirit. 2. Spiritual life--Christianity. 3. Weight loss--Religious aspects--Christianity. 4. Weight loss. I. Title.
  BV4501.3.D375 2008
  613.2'5--dc22

                              2008017850

Neither the publisher nor the author is engaged in rendering professional advice or services to the individual reader. The ideas, procedures, and suggestions in this book are not intended as a substitute for consulting with your physician. All matters regarding your health require medical supervision. Neither the author nor the publisher shall be liable or responsible for any loss or damage allegedly arising from any information or suggestion in this book.

While the author has made every effort to provide accurate telephone numbers and Internet addresses at the time of publication, neither the publisher nor the author assumes any responsibility for errors or for changes that occur after publication.

09 10 11 12 13 — 12 11 10 9 8 7
Printed in the United States of America

ONTENTS

Afterword

# INTRODUCTION

Dear friend, I pray that you may enjoy good health and that all may go well with you, even as your soul is getting along well.

—3 JOHN 2

A LITTLE OVER A decade ago, while serving on the faculty of the University of Illinois at Chicago, I began to work on the original version of *Spiritual Secrets to Weight Loss*. It had as its foundation my years of clinical experience combined with my study of the Scriptures with a focus on biblical precepts that are to govern Christian living. My working title was *The Fruit Diet* because it dealt with the fruits of the Spirit found in the Book of Galatians: love, joy, peace, patience, kindness, goodness, faithfulness, gentleness, and self-control (Gal. 5:22–23). I found that when we submit to the Holy Spirit, these nine character attributes are grown in us and we gain the help we need to change our lifestyles and improve our health.

Since the release of the original version, much has transpired. For one thing, I let my hair grow back, so for those of you who might own the first version, it's the same Kara Davis; I just look a little different. I also developed an eight-week class called "Weigh of Life" that, while biblically based, also incorporates practical information on diet, nutrition, and exercise. *Spiritual Secrets to Weight Loss: A 50-Day Renewal of Body, Mind, and Spirit* combines both the original version of *Spiritual Secrets* with the material from the "Weigh of Life" class.

I have deliberately chosen to forgo mentioning information in this introduction that is available through many other venues—information that most of us have heard repeatedly. So statistics and data on the prevalence of obesity and overweight, how it has become an epidemic over the past few decades, the health consequences related to excess body weight, the risk of premature death and disability, its impact on our children and adolescents, the astronomical costs associated with it both in health care dollars and through reduced productivity in the workplace, its psychological consequences and social stigmatization, and the stereotypes and discrimination that still prevail against obese and overweight people will not be covered here. While all of this is certainly important to know,

I believe by now most of us are aware of these things, at least to some degree. My omission of this information, however, does not mean I minimize it. We are presently in a health-care crisis as never experienced before. Future generations will suffer these health-related consequences to a greater extent than we have if nothing intervenes to halt current trends. What ought to shame us all is that this crisis is not the result of some unavoidable entity like an airborne virus, where disease may come upon us beyond our control. To the contrary, this crisis is by and large the result of personal choice. As I said in *Spiritual Secrets to Weight Loss*, we are digging our own graves, one forkful at a time.

So I acknowledge the epidemic confronting us, but I am omitting from this introduction the "gory" details. We have access to this information through all types of media, and I have also included an abundance of data and statistics in the Daily Facts/Tips segment. If, however, you desire specific information not included in this book, for instance, the role obesity plays in a form of cancer common to your family or the rate of obesity for your particular demographic group, then please seek the advice of your health care provider, inquire at your local library, or search the Internet. I am excited you have chosen to take part in this fifty-day journey, and I pray it will give you the inspiration and motivation you need to take charge of your lifestyle and improve your health.

Now I am going to take you through some of the basics of launching a new lifestyle of health and vitality by defining some important diet and health terminology, showing you the importance of an accountability partner and how to choose one, teaching some of the basics of diet and health, introducing the fifty-day covenant, pinpointing your chances for success, and much more. Are you ready? Well, let's get started!

Definition of Terms

It is important to have at least a rudimentary understanding of the terms commonly used in discussing diet and exercise. I would encourage you to use these definitions for only basic knowledge but to study other resources to broaden your understanding.

Calorie

A calorie is a unit used to measure the energy produced by food when it is oxidized ("burned up") in the body. Proteins and carbohydrates generate four calories for every gram; fat generates nine. Our daily caloric requirements vary based on age, gender, and activity level and should be adjusted if there is a case of being overweight or obese. Food and nutrition labels are calculated based on a two thousand–calorie diet. For weight loss, you will more than likely need to consume less. The USDA's "My Pyramid" Web site (www.mypyramid.gov) includes a calculator that can estimate your daily caloric requirement based on your age, gender, height, weight, and activity level.

Cholesterol

Cholesterol is a fatty substance your body needs to produce hormones and to maintain nerve cell function. The cholesterol in your blood is made by your liver, and you also get cholesterol by eating animal products like meat, eggs, and dairy foods. The two most important components of cholesterol are the LDL and the HDL. LDL cholesterol contributes to heart disease by leaving fatty deposits in the walls of the arteries. HDL cholesterol is beneficial. It actually removes extra cholesterol from the body.

Fats

Fats are essential for our health, but they have a bad reputation for many reasons. They have more calories per gram than carbohydrates and proteins, so we tend to associate them with being overweight or obese. Also, when we gain weight, we accumulate fat (adipose) tissue. We don't call overweight people "protein" or "carbohydrate"; we call them "fat." I believe this association has really tarnished the reputation of fats. It is true that some fats contribute to the risk for heart disease, but others actually protect against heart disease. All of them, however, generate nine calories per gram, so they should be consumed in moderation. Fats and oils contain varying quantities of the different types of fat. They are classified based on the major component.

Beneficial fats (lower LDL cholesterol; raise HDL cholesterol):

- Monounsaturated—found in olives and olive oil, canola oil, peanut oil, cashews, almonds, peanuts, avocados
- Polyunsaturated—found in corn, soybean, safflower and cottonseed oil, fish

Detrimental fats (raise LDL; trans fats lower HDL)

- Saturated—nonskim milk, butter, cheese, ice cream, meat, coconut
- Trans—margarines, partially hydrogenated vegetable oil, commercial baked goods and breading, deep fried chips

Proteins

Proteins are substances made up of units called amino acids. They are the building blocks for our bodies, making such tissue as muscle, skin, and blood. Protein is available through animal sources (e.g., meat, eggs, dairy) and plant sources (e.g., nuts, beans, whole grains).

Carbohydrates

Carbohydrates are the diverse category that makes up the majority of our diet. The common carbohydrate terminology of "simple" and "complex" can be misleading. Carbohydrates are made from the basic units of glucose, fructose, and galactose. They can be categorized in the following manner:

- Sugar: one or two units ("mono-" or "disaccharide")
- Starch: many units ("polysaccharide"), all digestible
- Fiber: many units ("polysaccharide"), all indigestible

  1. Soluble fiber (gummy texture)
  2. Insoluble fiber (coarse texture)

Fruits, vegetables, and grains are categorized as carbohydrates, although they may also contain protein and fat. Fruits and vegetables can be further categorized into the following:

- Crucifer family: broccoli, brussels sprouts, cauliflower, cabbage, greens (collards, mustard, kale), radishes, rutabaga, watercress, kohlrabi
- Melon/squash family: zucchini, pumpkin, cucumbers, acorn squash, butternut squash, honeydew melon, cantaloupe
- Legumes: beans, peas, alfalfa sprouts, lentils
- Solanum family: peppers, tomatoes, eggplant, potatoes
- Umbels: carrots, parsley, celery, parsnips

- Citrus family: lemon, grapefruit, limes, oranges, tangerines
- Lily family: asparagus, garlic, leeks, chives, onions, shallots

Grains have three components: the bran, the endosperm, and the germ. Whole grains maintain all three components. The refining process removes the bran and germ from the grain, and this also removes nutrients and fiber. Studies show that whole grain helps to protect against disease while refined grain may contribute to disease. Grains come in many different types other than wheat, oats, rice, and corn. Other less common grains include rye, barley, amaranth, buckwheat, quinoa, sorghum, millet, and triticale.

Vitamins and minerals

These are calorie-free nutrients your body cannot make that must be obtained from food or other sources. They are essential for the body's normal function as well as disease prevention.

Cardiometabolic exercise

This is also known as aerobic exercise. It is the type of exercise that increases your heart rate through continuous movement. Walking, swimming, jogging, dancing, skating, cycling, and some competitive sports are all forms of cardiometabolic exercise. They are beneficial in protecting against (or optimizing the control of) heart disease as well as some metabolic disorders like type 2 diabetes.

Strength training

This type of exercise focuses on strengthening muscles. Like cardiometabolic exercises, it is good for the heart, the circulation, and the metabolism. Unlike cardiometabolic exercise, it should not be done every day, but only two to three times per week.

Flexibility training

This is stretching, which will not protect against heart disease or diabetes but will help to protect the muscles against injury, and it certainly helps you to relax.

CHOOSING AN ACCOUNTABILITY PARTNER

Choosing and maintaining an accountability partner throughout the 50-Day Spiritual Secrets Renewal is crucial to your success in this program. Accountability is a biblical concept. Proverbs and Ecclesiastes both speak to this:

As iron sharpens iron, so one man sharpens another.

—Proverbs 27:17

Two are better than one, because they have a good return for their work: If one falls down, his friend can help him up. But pity the man who falls and has no one to help him up!

—Ecclesiastes 4:9–10

I strongly recommend you choose an accountability partner as the first order of business. While it may seem appropriate to restrict your selection to someone who is also setting out to lose weight, please don't limit yourself. What you should look for is someone who will encourage, motivate, and inspire you, and (most importantly) someone who will not shy away from issuing a word of correction when appropriate.

Jealousy grieves the Holy Spirit, but it is nevertheless a vice that abounds within the church community, so use discernment. (See Romans 13:13.) You don't want to make the mistake of being "accountable" to someone who might envy your success.

With so many ways to stay in touch, I'd suggest you be in contact with your accountability partner at least daily or every other day. Receiving an encouraging voice mail or an inspiring text message can make a world of difference. Obviously your relationship must be open enough that you are comfortable sharing your progress and pitfalls. It is important to make sure the person you select is a mature Christian who sincerely wants you to succeed and who cares enough about you to pray for you and with you.

EAT WELL. EAT LESS. MOVE MORE.

The premise for how we will achieve weight loss and better health is this: *eat well, eat less, move more.* Now, don't let the simplicity fool you. The current rate of obesity and overweight along with the many diseases related to improper diet and inadequate exercise prove that this concept is either easier said than done or it's blatantly ignored. This is hardly a novel idea. In fact, well over two thousand years ago, Hippocrates said, "If we could give every individual the right amount of nourishment and exercise, not too little and not too much, we would have found the safest way to health."[1] Really, there is nothing new under the sun.

Eat well.

This first precept refers to the quality of food. With research consistently demonstrating a connection between the types of food we eat and our health, there is truth to the adage, "You are what you eat." It seems every organ in the body is impacted by diet.

The range of diseases that are influenced by nutrition is broad, including cardiovascular disease, cancer, gastrointestinal diseases, osteoporosis, diabetes, arthritis, and dementia. The list goes on and on. Many people are aware of the impact diet has on the risk of cardiovascular disease and diabetes, but they fail to recognize how it influences our health outside of these conditions. And while cardiovascular disease and diabetes are highly prevalent, we can't ignore the role our diet plays in either protecting us against or hastening the development of a myriad of other illnesses.

The World Cancer Research Fund and the American Institute for Cancer Research released a report that details the ways we can reduce our risk for cancer through diet and exercise. Along with maintaining a normal BMI, the recommendations also include eating no more than eighteen ounces of red meat *per week* (not *per day*) with little processed meat, and limiting sodium and alcohol. In terms of our health as we grow older, studies continue to demonstrate a relationship between diet, cognitive function, and the ability to live independently in the elderly. Indeed, we are what we eat.

Eat less.

Eating less reflects the quantity of food. My husband tells me I have a tendency to take things for granted, especially when it comes to what people know about healthy living. So now I make a point of reminding people about things I'm prone to assume are obvious. One such reminder relates to serving sizes.

Understand that foods that are nutritionally sound and beneficial to our health must still be eaten in moderation! We are quick to concede that restriction is in order when it comes to "junk food," but we fail to recognize that excessive calories will lead to weight gain, even if the excess comes from foods that are an excellent source of nutrients. When it comes to weight gain, it is quite possible to have too much of a good thing. Portion control—limiting the *quantity* of food we eat—is crucial to achieving and maintaining weight loss. The American Dietetic Association (www.eatright.org) and the American Diabetes Association (www.diabetes.org) both have useful information on estimating serving sizes.

- Your fist is about the same size as one cup (8 ounces) of fruit.
- Your thumb (tip to base) is the size of one ounce of meat or cheese.
- The last section of your thumb (the tip) is about the same as 1 tablespoon.
- Your palm (minus fingers) equals three ounces of cooked meat, fish, or poultry.
- Your cupped hand equals one to two ounces of nuts or pretzels.[2]

Move more.
Finally, good health requires that we move more. Again, research confirms the connection between physical activity (or the lack thereof) and disease. As with diet, the impact of exercise on our health extends beyond the common conditions of cardiovascular disease and diabetes.

Currently, scientists attribute approximately 250,000 deaths per year in the United States to a lack of regular exercise. This number does not speak to the amount of chronic illness and disability that is a direct consequence of our sedentary lifestyles. Setting aside time for regular exercise and making a concerted effort to move more in our day-to-day routines are vitally important for our health and well-being.

BE A COVENANT KEEPER

During this fifty-day journey, I highly recommend that you and your accountability partner or group make a commitment to follow the Spiritual Secrets to Weight Loss 50-Day Covenant. As part of the covenant, I have included some very basic guidelines for diet and exercise. In terms of what you can or cannot eat, I have not listed specific foods, so there is much flexibility within the confines of the covenant.

At the conclusion of each week during your fifty-day renewal, I have included an assessment for you to chart how well you are keeping your covenant. This weekly assessment is not to put any legalistic restraints on your progress, but it will provide a point of discussion when you meet with your accountability partner or small group. The "Victories" and "Pitfalls" sections will help identify what circumstances help motivate you to eat well and exercise as well as what causes you to binge or not exercise. You will be more aware than ever of what you eat and how to avoid certain triggers that take you off track for your goal of getting healthier.

I would encourage you to make time for learning about nutrition, exercise, and even how to prepare meals in a healthy way. These changes are intended to be permanent, and the more you know about a healthy lifestyle, the easier it is to live one. I've subscribed to *Cooking Light* magazine for years and find their articles on nutrition and exercise to be relevant, up-to-date, and easy to read. They also have great recipes. With a working knowledge on healthy living, you will find that you willingly maintain a covenant for a healthy life well beyond the fifty days.

"Do Diet Plans Work?"

It seems that as the prevalence of obesity and overweight has increased, we've seen the number of diet plans increase in a parallel fashion. The heavier we get, the more options we have at our disposal. Choose your weapon: low fat, low carb, high fat, high carb, liquids or solids, carnivore or vegan, and do you add a supplement or do you refrain? What gives?

If you haven't guessed by my tone, I am not a big fan of diet plans. And my lack of enthusiasm for them does not stem from any lack of efficacy. To the contrary, I am the first to say that diet plans do indeed work. They work if you follow them. In a 2005 study published in the *Journal of the American Medical Association* comparing the Atkins, Ornish, Weight Watchers, and Zone diets, the investigators found:

> Each popular diet modestly reduced body weight and several cardiac risk factors at one year. Overall dietary adherence rates were low, although increased adherence was associated with greater weight loss and cardiac risk factor reductions for each diet group.[3]

If you stick with a weight loss plan, it will work, but most people don't stick with them. That is one of the reasons I don't recommend them, because too often they become a lesson in futility and a source of great frustration. But beyond that, food is for our enjoyment. Eating ought not to be a highly regimented experience. Yes, we practice self-control with our eating habits, but this does not mean we forfeit spontaneity and variety. Likewise, food preferences are deeply rooted, reflecting cultural, ethnic, and family traditions. These nuances are generally not taken into consideration when diet plans are created.

I believe one of the most effective components in structured diet plans is the requirement for accountability. This, as I mentioned, is a biblical concept to which we should adhere. But keep in mind you don't need to follow a structured meal plan in order to be held accountable to someone else. The purpose of an accountability partner is not so much to check the amount of fat you've eaten relative to carbohydrates but to persuade you to resist temptation, to encourage you to subject your flesh, to intercede in prayer for you, and to reprove you when you are careless.

Certainly, if you are determined to try a particular diet plan and it is safe, then go ahead and use it in conjunction with this fifty-day renewal. One does not preclude the other. I would hope, however, that long before we reach day fifty, you discover that the Word of God and the indwelling Holy Spirit are truly sufficient to guide you as you implement lifestyle changes for better health.

"WHAT ARE MY CHANCES FOR LONG-TERM SUCCESS?"

Your chances for long-term success will depend on your definition of *success*. But for our purposes and since research has shown that even modest amounts of weight loss confer health benefits, we will define success in terms of improved health rather than personal goals. R. R. Wing and J. O. Hill have proposed long-term success as "intentionally losing at least 10 percent of initial body weight and keeping it off for at least one year."[4] Under these terms, approximately 20 percent of overweight and obese people are able to achieve success. While this is a far cry from 100 percent, it is still much more encouraging than the dismally low 2 percent success rate we've heard in recent years.

This definition, however, probably does not line up with what you have set as a personal goal. If, for instance, you are 5 feet 6 inches, and your present weight is 250 pounds, then "success" under these terms would mean you bring your weight down to 225 pounds and maintain it for at least a year. Both weights, however, meet the criteria for obesity. At 250 pounds, the body mass index or BMI is 40.3, which is stage 3 obesity. At

225 pounds, the BMI is 36.3, which is stage 2 obesity. At first glance, this seems hardly a reason to celebrate. Wouldn't real success be to reach a BMI within the normal range, which for this height would be 155 pounds or less? How on earth could we consider someone who is still obese as being successful? But we *can* if we keep our focus on health, since there are proven health benefits with even modest degrees of weight loss.

The other reason we will focus on health rather than personal goals is so that it will help to keep our motives pure. Our personal goals are usually just that—personal. Let's be honest; they are often based on such things as a desired clothing size, attractiveness to the opposite sex, and wanting to avoid embarrassment at high school reunions. We become egocentric, even narcissistic, when we set out to lose weight. And if we thoroughly examine our hearts, we might find that even when our concern is toward improving our health, the motives can still be quite selfish: *I* want to lose weight because *I'm* tired of taking pills, *I'm* tired of going to the doctor, *I'm* tired of spending so much money on medications, *I'm* tired of having aching joints and being fatigued, and *I* want to prove to everyone that *I* can do better!

But God is never glorified through self-centeredness. So we ought to set a goal to honor Him by being excellent stewards of our bodies, His temple. We ought to set a goal to honor Him through living in a manner that reflects His attributes of discipline, self-control, temperance, prudence, and sobriety. We ought to honor Him by being steadfast in resisting the temptations that surround us. I suggest making these things the primary goal and setting a 10 percent weight reduction as the secondary goal, achieving the latter by losing two to three pounds per week. If the initial 10 percent finds the BMI still in the obese or overweight range, then set a subsequent goal of 10 percent only after maintaining the initial weight loss for several months to a year.

Ideally, the 10 percent reduction should come by way of permanent lifestyle modification. The quantity of food, the quality of food, and the activity level should all change for the better. For some, however, prescription medications or bariatric surgery may be reasonable options in conjunction with lifestyle changes to help secure success. These are discussed in more detail during week six.

BASIC NUTRITION AND EXERCISE GUIDELINES

Believe it or not, lifestyle modification is not rocket science! We can't allow ourselves to become intimidated at the thought of learning and implementing a few changes for better health. Yes, there is a natural fear of the unknown, and there is comfort with the familiar, but if "familiar" habits are destroying your health and the health of your children, then it is time to learn some new things and not be apprehensive about it. With that in mind and with a desire to keep things uncomplicated, our approach will begin with seven very simple pieces of advice.

1. Your diet should be comprised primarily of plant-based foods. Somehow, the concept became ingrained into American culture that meat is the "main course" and plant-based foods are "side items." Reverse this line of thinking. Reduce your intake of meat, especially meats that are processed, smoked, dried, and salted. Plant-based foods such as whole grains, vegetables, legumes, seeds, nuts, and fruits should constitute the majority of your diet.

2. Spend more time in your kitchen. In other words, cook more often so that you eat out less often. It is extremely hard to maintain control of what you eat if you do not prepare it yourself. Currently, there are 925,000 restaurants in America, and one out of five meals is eaten outside of the home. We cannot control important things like the sodium, saturated fat, and calorie content of our meals with this much eating out. The colossal serving sizes from full-service and fast-food restaurants only persuade us to ignore satiety cues. I believe it is close to impossible to experience long-term success with weight loss unless there are tight restrictions on ordering out, eating out, taking out, having it delivered, or driving through.

3. Watch your beverages. As we will discuss on day thirty-two, beverages often go overlooked in calorie counting. If you aren't careful, you can accumulate hundreds of empty calories each day through what you choose to drink. A recent study found that even diet soda was associated with the development of the metabolic syndrome, a finding that clearly warrants further study.[5]

4. Limit, LIMIT, *LIMIT* the amount of sugary and salty snacks you eat or allow your children to eat. Since these types of foods are heavily advertised, you will need to make a habit of turning off the television—a practice that

promotes good health in and of itself. Snacks have their role; just make sure what you choose is beneficial and not detrimental.

5. Stop going for seconds. Enough said.

6. Stop putting enough food for seconds on your first plate. Enough said.

7. Exercise regularly (aim for sixty minutes, most days of the week), but also look for other opportunities to move—and be diligent about it. For instance, unless you are physically disabled, there is really no need to hunt for a parking space close to the entrance of the store. In doing so, you are denying yourself a much-needed opportunity to move. Likewise, taking the elevator instead of the stairs and driving to places close enough to walk are habits so ingrained in our culture that we don't give them a second thought. That is why we must make a conscientious effort to do otherwise.

Seven rules, with seven being the number of completion. If you carefully adhere to these seven pieces of advice, you will see results. But there is something in addition to this advice that we must be cognizant of, and that is the connection between the mind, body, and spirit.

BODY, MIND, AND SPIRIT CONNECTION

The Bible confirms the connection between the mind and the body. In recent years, we have seen the scientific community affirm this relationship in studies demonstrating the detrimental effects of such things as depression and stress on our physical well-being. The Book of Proverbs is replete with verses attesting to the physical, emotional, mental, and spiritual bond:

A cheerful heart is good medicine, but a crushed spirit dries up the bones.

—Proverbs 17:22

A happy heart makes the face cheerful, but heartache crushes the spirit.

—Proverbs 15:13

A cheerful look brings joy to the heart, and good news gives
health to the bones.

—Proverbs 15:30

Pleasant words are a honeycomb, sweet to the soul and healing
to the bones.

—Proverbs 16:24

A man's spirit sustains him in sickness, but a crushed spirit
who can bear?

—Proverbs 18:14

We must not only appreciate the many facets of our total being, but
we must also understand their connection when we set out to make lifestyle changes for better health. Consider this: in all likelihood, the seven
rules just covered are, at the very least, familiar if not common knowledge
to most reading this book. I rarely encounter a patient whose response
is one of total ignorance when I review the things they should be doing
to improve their health. Granted, some may not know the specifics, and
they may lack a comprehensive understanding, but a grasp of the basic
precepts is evident. I have yet to encounter the person who says, "You
don't say! I never knew I should be doing that!" when I suggest they eat
more vegetables than they do ice cream.

So then, if we already know what we *should* be doing, then clearly
there is something hindering the implementation. The pursuit for what
hinders is exactly what drives us to try one diet plan after the next and
to join one health club after the next. It seems we expect this hindering
force will be revealed and dealt a mortal blow once we're able to connect
with the perfect diet plan or health club. But this is not how it works.
The hindering force is part of our nature. So while it *must* be neutralized, it *can't* be neutralized by trying the latest technique for losing
weight or through joining a popular health club. If we fail to appreciate
the mind, body, and spirit connection and fail to acknowledge the role
of our emotions and the powerful influence of our flesh nature, then our
efforts will be futile.

First, let's examine the emotions. Some unhealthy habits are fueled by
the state of our emotions. Depression, for instance, drains us of the motivation and energy required for regular exercise. It also has a great effect
on eating behaviors. Some people lose their appetites, and others overeat.

About half of people with binge-eating disorder are clinically depressed, and the psychiatric disorders of anorexia nervosa and bulimia nervosa relate, of course, to eating patterns. But even when there is no binging and no criteria for making the diagnosis of anorexia or bulimia, depression still impedes our ability to make long-term lifestyle changes.

Anxiety is another emotion that will hinder our progress. Smoking, excessive alcohol consumption, and overeating are very common among those who are under high levels of stress or are anxious.

Rejection is another powerful emotion that is often self-medicated with food—especially those foods that are "comforting."

Along with emotions, we also have a flesh nature. It is the flesh nature that drives us to indulgence, excess, and gluttony. The flesh nature compels us to ignore the God-given sensation of genuine hunger and persuades us to eat in response to the sight, smell, taste, and availability of food—whether we are hungry or not. Food advertisers target our flesh nature through catchy slogans. Certainly you should "have it your way" and "obey your thirst," because the bottom line is you really "can't stop eating 'em." And the flesh, once satisfied, will always respond with a contented, "I'm lovin' it."

The influence of negative emotions and the flesh nature will override the best plans for weight loss. This is why recognizing the connection between the body, mind, and spirit is so crucial. But beyond acknowledging the connection, there must also be a renewal, and this is the foundation for *Spiritual Secrets to Weight Loss: A 50-Day Renewal of Body, Mind, and Spirit.* As a Christian, I believe when we accept through faith the atoning work of Jesus Christ, we then are indwelt by the Holy Spirit. Our bodies become His temple, and through the work of the Holy Spirit we are transformed into new creatures. This transformation brings with it a renewing of the mind, whereby we are no longer powerless when it comes to our flesh nature. We are no longer subject to the inclinations of our emotions. Instead, the Christian is privileged to completely submit to the leading of the Holy Spirit. Inherent to the Spirit's nature are the very character traits required for permanent lifestyle change. This means self-control, discipline, moderation, and sobriety are not only within the realm of possibility, but they actually reflect who we are in Christ as well. As we mature in the things of God, we will find that the mind, body, and spirit connection is indeed a blessing and not a curse.

I am excited that you have decided to take this fifty-day journey, and I pray you will gain insight and knowledge with each day. I am thankful for the opportunity to serve you, and I give God the glory for the things He has done.

Let's get started right now by making a covenant toward good health!

—Kara Davis, MD

SPIRITUAL SECRETS TO WEIGHT LOSS
50-DAY COVENANT

SETTING THE FOUNDATION FOR A HEALTHIER LIFE

At the end of the ten days they looked healthier and better nourished than any of the young men who ate the royal food.

—DANIEL 1:15

NUTRITION AND EATING

- Set and maintain specific mealtimes for breakfast, lunch, and dinner.
- Eat only in "food rooms" (kitchen, dining room, office break room).
- Do not watch television during meals.
- Eat fast food no more than once weekly.
- Do not eat or drink while commuting.
- Drink only water, coffee (no lattes), tea, and skim milk. Avoid soft drinks.
- Limit food quantity to a single serving with modest portions.
- Choose high-fiber carbohydrates, including vegetables, fruits, whole grains, and legumes.
- Choose lean proteins including fish and skinless, white-meat poultry.
- Select whole-grain foods over refined grains.
- Eat a nutritious breakfast each morning.
- Avoid highly processed foods and beverages, especially those containing high fructose corn syrup, refined flour, or trans fats.
- Avoid excessive sugar and sodium.

ACTIVITY*

- Walk or do other cardiometabolic exercise daily (minimum thirty minutes, ideally forty-five to sixty minutes).
- Strength train two to three times per week.
- Take in no more than one hour each day of *seated leisure* screen time (e.g., television, video games, non–work related computer time).
- Make a diligent and concerted effort to *MOVE MORE.*
- Get an adequate amount of sleep.

SPIRITUAL

- Pray daily, specifically for lifestyle-related issues.
- Intercede for your accountability partner.
- Daily read the Bible and spend time in devotions.
- Attend church regularly.

I, _____ (insert your name), do hereby make a covenant with God, my family, my community, and my future generations to take on the full commitment of the Spiritual Secrets to Weight Loss 50-Day Covenant. I pledge to make every effort with God's help to make this a permanent lifestyle these fifty days and beyond.

Signed,

_____

Date _____

---

*Please check with your physician prior to implementing an exercise program.

BODY MASS INDEX FOR ADULTS TABLE

	NORMAL						OVERWEIGHT					OBESE									
BMI	19	20	21	22	23	24	25	26	27	28	29	30	31	32	33	34	35	36	37	38	39
HEIGHT (INCHES)	BODY WEIGHT (POUNDS)																				
58	91	96	100	105	110	115	119	124	129	134	138	143	148	153	158	162	167	172	177	181	186
59	94	99	104	109	114	119	124	128	133	138	143	148	153	158	163	168	173	178	183	188	193
60	97	102	107	112	118	123	128	133	138	143	148	153	158	163	168	174	179	184	189	194	199
61	100	106	111	116	122	127	132	137	143	148	153	158	164	169	174	180	185	190	195	201	206
62	104	109	115	120	126	131	136	142	147	153	158	164	169	175	180	186	191	196	202	207	213
63	107	113	118	124	130	135	141	146	152	158	163	169	175	180	186	191	197	203	208	214	220
64	110	116	122	128	134	140	145	151	157	163	169	174	180	186	192	197	204	209	215	221	227
65	114	120	126	132	138	144	150	156	162	168	174	180	186	192	198	204	210	216	222	228	234
66	118	124	130	136	142	148	155	161	167	173	179	186	192	198	204	210	216	223	229	235	241
67	121	127	134	140	146	153	159	166	172	178	185	191	198	204	211	217	223	230	236	242	249
68	125	131	138	144	151	158	164	171	177	184	190	197	203	210	216	223	230	236	243	249	256
69	128	135	142	149	155	162	169	176	182	189	196	203	209	216	223	230	236	243	250	257	263
70	132	139	146	153	160	167	174	181	188	195	202	209	216	222	229	236	243	250	257	264	271
71	136	143	150	157	165	172	179	186	193	200	208	215	222	229	236	243	250	257	265	272	279
72	140	147	154	162	169	177	184	191	199	206	213	221	228	235	242	250	258	265	272	279	287
73	144	151	159	166	174	182	189	197	204	212	219	227	235	242	250	257	265	272	280	288	295
74	148	155	163	171	179	186	194	202	210	218	225	233	241	249	256	264	272	280	287	295	303
75	152	160	168	176	184	192	200	208	216	224	232	240	248	256	264	272	279	287	295	303	311
76	156	164	172	180	189	197	205	213	221	230	238	246	254	262	271	279	287	295	304	312	320

	EXTREME OBESITY														
BMI	40	41	42	43	44	45	46	47	48	49	50	51	52	53	54
HEIGHT (INCHES)	BODY WEIGHT (POUNDS)														
58	191	196	201	205	210	215	220	224	229	234	239	244	248	253	258
59	198	203	208	212	217	222	227	232	237	242	247	252	257	262	267
60	204	209	215	220	225	230	235	240	245	250	255	261	266	271	276
61	211	217	222	227	232	238	243	248	254	259	264	269	275	280	285
62	218	224	229	235	240	246	251	256	262	267	273	278	284	289	295
63	225	231	237	242	248	254	259	265	270	278	282	287	293	299	304
64	232	238	244	250	256	262	267	273	279	285	291	296	302	308	314
65	240	246	252	258	264	270	276	282	288	294	300	306	312	318	324
66	247	253	260	266	272	278	284	291	297	303	309	315	322	328	334
67	255	261	268	274	280	287	293	299	306	312	319	325	331	338	344
68	262	269	276	282	289	295	302	308	315	322	328	335	341	348	354
69	270	277	284	291	297	304	311	318	324	331	338	345	351	358	365
70	278	285	292	299	306	313	320	327	334	341	348	355	362	369	376
71	286	293	301	308	315	322	329	338	343	351	358	365	372	379	386
72	294	302	309	316	324	331	338	346	353	361	368	375	383	390	397
73	302	310	318	325	333	340	348	355	363	371	378	386	393	401	408
74	311	319	326	334	342	350	358	365	373	381	389	396	404	412	420
75	319	327	335	343	351	359	367	375	383	391	399	407	415	423	431
76	328	336	344	353	361	369	377	385	394	402	410	418	426	435	443

BMI Categories

- Underweight = < 18.5
- Normal weight = 18.5–24.9
- Overweight = 25–29.9
- Obesity I = 30–34.9
- Obesity II = 35–39.9
- Obesity III = 40>

Courtesy of National Heart, Lung, and Blood Institute, National Institutes of Health

Know God

DAY **ONE**

STARTING OUT WITH GOD

*In reply Jesus declared, "I tell you the truth, no one can see
the kingdom of God unless he is born again."*

—JOHN 3:3

YOU MIGHT THINK it strange that a book devoted to weight loss
would begin week one with a portion of the conversation that
took place between Jesus and Nicodemus. But I think it is
imperative that we, as physician/author and reader, start this journey on
the "same page," so to speak. The best time to determine whether we are in
agreement is here at day one.

I have a wealth of experience in treating and counseling men and
women who are overweight or obese in my role as a physician and also
in my role as a pastor's wife. One tendency I find far more often than
I'd like is that some people are willing to try *anything* that promises
success. Some weight loss plans are totally irrational but will nevertheless convince highly intelligent people to forsake their common sense in
the hope of reaching their weight loss goal.

Unfortunately, capitalism is the primary motivator for many in the
weight loss industry. The dieter's success is less a priority than the plan's
ability to generate cash flow. So the bogus plan is made available to an
extremely large consumer base (with now roughly two-thirds of the adult
population being overweight[1]) who is easily captivated by the promise of
weight loss. Even though the plan may not be harmful, there is little proof,
if any, to validate its claims. More often than not, it doesn't work.

But, oddly enough, the failure of one plan does not seem to make us
skeptical about trying another. While you might assume that after being
burned by Plan A, there would be a measure of caution and suspicion
about Plan B, this does not seem to be the case. In fact, the weight-loss
industry continues to thrive, though statistics show a dismally low record
of success. One would think that after spending billions of dollars year
after year on weight loss, we would not find ourselves in the middle of

an obesity epidemic. But here we are, and still, the weight loss industry continues to thrive.

That being said, I have selected John 3:3 as the verse to start this Spiritual Secrets 50-Day Renewal. In the third chapter of John, Nicodemus, a Pharisee, comes to Jesus by night and acknowledges that Jesus is a teacher sent from God. Jesus responds to him with our verse for the day, John 3:3. I believe this passage of scripture makes our purpose crystal clear. The foundation for this journey to renewal does not rest in what you eat and how much you exercise. The foundation rests in having faith in Jesus Christ, in being "born again."

Being "born again" is not about church attendance or having a strong sense of morality, although these things should be evident in the lives of believers. But the new birth that Jesus described to Nicodemus involves a personal, faith-based relationship with Jesus Christ; a relationship that serves to make us justified before God the Father.   This   relationship comes by way of confession and repentance, and it opens the door for us to receive forgiveness of our sins through the undefiled blood that Jesus shed on the cross—blood that provided the full payment of the debt we owed as a consequence of our sinfulness. When we are born again, the Bible says we're new: "Therefore, if anyone is in Christ, he is a new creation; the old has gone, the new has come!" (2 Cor. 5:17). It is this "newness" that plants in us the desire to live in a way that is pleasing to God and in accordance with His precepts.

If all this is familiar to you and describes who you are, then you and I are indeed on the same page! I trust you will find this fifty-day journey to be quite refreshing. I hope to encourage and motivate you to make life-style changes for weight loss and better health.

If, however, this all sounds foreign, then I would encourage you to continue this daily journey with the hope that God would take your desire for optimal *physical* health and reveal the need for you to optimize your *spiritual* health. More importantly, I would encourage you to read the Bible for yourself and find a Bible-teaching church in your area where the pastor and membership can help you to understand the love of Jesus Christ in a face-to-face encounter.

Yes, one of my purposes in writing *Spiritual Secrets to Weight Loss* is to help you lose weight for better health. But my number-one desire for you is not so much that you lose weight but that you have a right relationship with God, a relationship that is contingent upon accepting the sacrifice of His Son, Jesus Christ. I'd much rather you be obese and born again than have a perfect BMI and not know the Lord.

Also in the Book of John, we are given an account of the last Passover meal Jesus shared with His disciples prior to His arrest and crucifixion. He used their time together to instruct them on things to come and to give them the assurance of the Holy Spirit:

> If you love me, you will obey what I command. And I will ask the Father, and he will give you another Counselor to be with you forever—the Spirit of truth. The world cannot accept him, because it neither sees him nor knows him. But you know him, for he lives with you and will be in you.
>
> —John 14:15–17

Christians, along with having our sins forgiven, are also indwelt by the Holy Spirit. It is this very Spirit of God who gives us what we need to live out our calling as disciples of Christ. He first fills us with a desire to manifest our status of "new creatures" in our day-to-day living. Then He equips us, empowers us, and reveals to us what is hindering us so that we're able to lead a victorious lifestyle, not just in our eating and exercise habits, but also in everything we do. This gives God glory. My goal is to effectively convey to you that, through the truth of God's Word and the powerful help of the Holy Spirit, you already have what you need to take charge of your lifestyle and improve your health. That being said, let's begin our journey.

Daily Prayer

Father, I am eternally grateful for Your love toward me in that You sacrificed Your Son, Jesus Christ, so that I might have eternal life. I begin this fifty-day journey with a heart of thanksgiving for Your saving grace and for Your indwelling Spirit. Now I pray that You open my heart and mind to receive the transforming power of Your Word, and I thank You for success on my journey.

HEALTH FACT OF THE DAY
DAY ONE

The prevalence of obesity and being overweight is higher for Christians than for any other religious group. Atheists even weigh less than born-again believers.[2]

JEHOVAH-RAPHE:
THE GOD WHO HEALS YOU

I am the LORD your God, who brought you out of Egypt, out of the land of slavery. You shall have no other gods before me.

—EXODUS 20:2–3

I N THE BOOK of Exodus, the Lord reveals Himself as Jehovah-Raphe, the Lord God our Healer. God describes Himself in this manner after establishing a covenant with the Israelites. They had just experienced a miraculous deliverance from centuries of slavery in Egypt, even witnessing the destruction of the Egyptian army in the Red Sea. With high spirits they praised God, but in a few days they found themselves facing a challenge: "Then Moses led Israel from the Red Sea, and they went out into the wilderness of Shur; and they went three days in the wilderness and found no water" (Exod. 15:22, NAS). They then traveled to Marah, where they discovered the water was too bitter to drink. Rather than respond in faith, they grumbled and complained to Moses, who sought the Lord for an answer. The Lord not only provided the solution, but He also established a covenant:

> Then Moses cried out to the LORD, and the LORD showed him a piece of wood. He threw it into the water, and the water became sweet. There [at Marah] the LORD made a decree and a law for them, and there he tested them. He said, "If you listen carefully to the voice of the LORD your God and do what is right in his eyes, if you pay attention to his commands and keep all his decrees, I will not bring on you any of the diseases I brought on the Egyptians, for I am the LORD, who heals you."
>
> —Exodus 15:25–26

26

What a wonderful reality to know God is our Healer! Even His name, Jehovah-Raphe, speaks of His desire to heal. But since this particular name was revealed in the context of a covenant, I think it is important—rather, imperative—that we understand the concept of covenant.

Covenants are promises, sealed agreements made between two parties. There are several covenants established in the Bible, and they can be categorized into two types: unconditional and conditional. An unconditional covenant has no terms attached. An example would be the covenant God established with Noah after the Flood, when He promised to never again destroy the earth by water. (See Genesis 9:15.) So, in spite of mankind's sinfulness, we can be certain that there will never be another worldwide flood.

Other covenants, such as the one we find here in Exodus 15, start with the word *if*. These are conditional covenants. They have stipulations that must be met by one or both parties in order for the agreement to be legitimate. When God revealed Himself as Jehovah-Raphe, it was in this context. The passage makes it clear that the Israelites had to meet certain requirements in order to experience God as a healer. These conditions were the following:

- Listen carefully to the Lord.
- Do what is right in His eyes.
- Pay attention to His commands.
- Keep all His decrees (or statutes).

If they abided by these requirements, then God promised to spare them from experiencing the diseases He had brought on the Egyptians. If they failed to do so, then they could not rest in the assurance that He would manifest Himself as Jehovah-Raphe and provide them with healing.

Some Bible scholars compare the land of Egypt to our world system with all its bondage and sinful values. The Israelites' deliverance from Egypt is symbolic of our salvation through Christ. After the first Passover, Egypt was never again "home" to the Israelites. Likewise, after salvation, the world is no longer "home" to the born-again believer: "As it is, you do not belong to the world, but I [Jesus] have chosen you out of the world." (John 15:19). While we were once held captive as slaves to sin, we have now been miraculously liberated through the redeeming power of Christ.

If Egypt symbolizes the world, what would be the modern-day "diseases of the Egyptians"? They would be diseases that result from a disregard of the conditions set by God when He made the promise to be a healer. Keep in mind, the Exodus 15 covenant is conditional. If sickness is the consequence of our willful disregard of the covenant's terms, then we really have no assurance that our bodies will be healed.

For the sake of our health, we must strive to be covenant keepers. A covenant keeper would not intentionally commit the sin of idolatry. A covenant keeper would not willfully and habitually yield to the lusts of the flesh. Doing such would violate the conditions that God established for healing.

In a spiritual sense, addiction—whether to tobacco, alcohol, drugs, or even food—is a form of idolatry. The addict yields allegiance to a *substance*, giving it authority to control his behavior. That authority belongs only to God. The substance, then, fits the definition of an idol—something that exerts control over us, something that is passionately pursued and even worshiped. Our modern-day idols are not the statues and figurines of Old Testament times; they are such things as money, power, and substances. The Bible is clear that only God should control us, and only God should be worshiped.

Certainly any form of idolatry would violate the conditions set by Jehovah-Raphe. And we see evidence of this in the "diseases of Egypt" that plague us today. Close to one million deaths per year are potentially preventable and are the consequences of lifestyle choices and addiction. In 2000 tobacco accounted for 435,000 deaths (18.1 percent of total deaths in the United States), poor diet and physical inactivity accounted for 365,000 deaths (15.2 percent of the total), and excessive alcohol consumption accounted for 85,000 deaths (3.5 percent of the total). And while smoking remains the leading cause of preventable death, if current trends continue, improper diet and inadequate exercise will soon gain the lead.[1, 2]

Yes, we live in a fallen world where disease and death are unavoidable. When affliction strikes, we ought to cry out to Jehovah-Raphe for mercy. But let the cry come from the lips of a covenant keeper. We must break the tendency of expecting God to operate on *our* terms and instead live by *His* terms. The Holy Spirit enables us to adhere to the conditions required for healing. As we learn to yield to Him, we will enter into the benefits of healing as promised in the Scriptures.

Daily Prayer

I thank You, Lord, for Your covenant promises. Your Word assures me that You do not have the capacity to lie, and I know

You can only speak truth. I am able to believe Your promises because of who You are. Please renew a spirit within me of trust and obedience so that I will be a faithful covenant keeper.

HEALTH FACT OF THE DAY

DAY TWO

Drinking a single 150-calorie can of soda per day will add up to fifteen extra pounds over a year's time.

I want to be controlled by God — not food

THE GOD OF LOVE

So whether you eat or drink or whatever you do,
do it all for the glory of God.

—1 CORINTHIANS 10:31

I N CASE YOU haven't figured it out by now, the "secret" in *Spiritual Secrets to Weight Loss* is really no secret at all but is plainly presented throughout the Bible. As the apostle Paul confirms in today's Scripture verse, our purpose is to glorify God in everything we do. This is the secret! When this becomes our passion, we'll experience health and well-being in every aspect of our lives—the spiritual, the emotional, and even the physical.

We glorify God in many ways—through our obedience, in worship, with praise, and so on. We certainly give Him glory when we live out His attributes. The Holy Spirit is who empowers us to manifest the nature of God. He equips us to take authority over our thoughts, attitudes, and actions so that they are in keeping with God's character.

A key attribute of God is love. First John 4:16 says, "God is love. Whoever lives in love lives in God, and God in him." The first fruit of the Spirit is love (Gal. 5:22). And we are identified as children of God by our love for one another (1 John 3:10).

But keep in mind, love bears evidence that goes beyond kind words or a warm smile. The evidence of love is sacrifice. We see this in John 3:16, one of the most widely quoted verses in the Bible: "For God so loved the world that he gave his one and only Son, that whoever believes in him shall not perish but have eternal life." God manifested His love through sacrifice—He *gave*. Yes, I am encouraged by God's kind words to me, and I rejoice that His smile is upon me, but the real *evidence* of His love is that He sacrificed His Son for me.

If we are to glorify God through love, then there ought to be evidence of that love in the form of a sacrificial life. But this presents a challenge because we live in an egocentric world where selfishness, rather than sacrifice, is the order of the day. We are constantly encouraged to set ourselves as our first priority and to gratify our own desires above the needs of others. This is contrary to sacrificial love. If we fail to diligently reject this pattern of the world, we will find our "love" reduced to an empty confession, bearing little evidence.

I once took care of a man who smoked cigarettes heavily. On one particular visit, his wife stayed in the room with us during his appointment. After I counseled him (again!) on the detrimental effects of smoking, he gave me his routine answer, "OK, Doc, I'll try to quit." Then his wife broke down in tears. She accused him of not loving her because she felt if he truly loved her, he wouldn't behave as if he were determined to make her a widow. For her, his affirmations of love had become lip service since the *evidence* of love would have required that he *sacrifice* his cigarettes in order to meet her need. *Love* is an action word, and the action is sacrifice. The Bible says, "Let us not love with words or tongue but with actions and in truth" (1 John 3:18).

The number one cause of preventable death is tobacco. But the combination of improper diet and inadequate exercise runs a close second and is expected to take the lead if current trends continue. Obesity has a substantial effect on our mortality, reducing the length of life by five to twenty years for people who are severely obese.[1] Now that it has become so prevalent in our youth, it's expected that obesity-related disability will skyrocket in the near future as these young people become adults, since their bodies would have been subjected to the detrimental effects for a greater number of years.[2]

That being said, let's reconsider God's attribute of sacrificial love, keeping in mind that we glorify God through the manifestation of His character in our daily living. Because God loved us, He sacrificed His only Son for our sakes. What, then, are *we* willing to sacrifice for the sake of those *we* love? Remember, it is not enough to profess love; we are called to show it.

Regular exercise will improve our health and increase the years we're able to live independently. Are we making the sacrifice of regular exercise to show love to our families in a tangible way? Our food choices have a profound impact on our long-term health. Do we keep our loved ones in mind when we decide what we will or will not eat? Are we willing to break bad habits (no matter how much we enjoy them!) so that the people we care about won't be burdened by the diseases and disability we've brought on ourselves? When we willfully and perpetually overeat, when we willfully and perpetually choose a sedentary lifestyle, are we mindful of the impact our choices will have on those we profess to love?

Love is sacrificial. God set the example of His love for us in the life and death of Jesus Christ. The cross is where He demonstrated that true love is manifested in sacrifice. So how do we measure up when it comes to imitating God? Are we glorifying Him by imitating His attribute of love? Or do we give our "loved ones" lip service. If God's love for us was so great that He sacrificed His Son, then shouldn't we be willing to sacrifice something on a much smaller scale for those we love? Refusing to eat a second serving of mashed potatoes is a small sacrifice. Breaking the television habit in order to cook healthy meals is a small sacrifice. Taking a walk is a small sacrifice.

We are called to give God glory, and we do this through love—sacrificial love. Let's examine our lives and purpose to love, not just in word but also in action. Show your love by making some sacrifices for better health.

Daily Prayer

Father, I thank You for the sacrifice of Your Son, Jesus Christ, and I thank You for giving me this same capacity to love through the fruit of the Spirit. Now, Lord, I ask that You quicken in me the desire to show love to others by relinquishing those habits and tendencies that are detrimental to my health.

HEALTH FACT OF THE DAY
DAY THREE

For men in their seventies, a healthy lifestyle that includes weight management, blood pressure control, smoking abstinence, and regular exercise not only increased the probability of survival to age ninety, but was also associated with a lower incidence of chronic disease and better physical function and mental well-being during the later years of life.[3]

DAY **FOUR**

JEHOVAH-JIREH: THE GOD WHO PROVIDES

Then God said, "I give you every seed-bearing plant on the face of the whole earth and every tree that has fruit with seed in it. They will be yours for food. And to all the beasts of the earth and all the birds of the air and all the creatures that move on the ground—everything that has the breath of life in it—I give every green plant for food." And it was so.
—GENESIS 1:29–30

F I WERE asked to list the many ways that God shows His love and mercy toward us, meeting our nutritional needs would be placed near the top. In the first chapter of the Book of Genesis, we see this goodness of God manifested. In the process of Creation, when God spoke everything into existence, we find the following sequence of events:

DAY:	EVENT
1	Light was created
2	The separation of water from sky
3	The separation of water from dry land; the land produces vegetation
4	The separation of day and night
5	Birds and sea (water) animals created
6	Land animals created; the creation of man
7	Rest

Notice there was an order to Creation, and the order was structured in such a way that all of mankind's *needs* were in place prior to our existence. In Genesis 1:11, God speaks a word upon the land to produce "seed-bearing plants and trees on the land that bear fruit with seed in it, according to their various kinds." The mandate given to the earth was to provide us with a wide variety of food—and it was good.

Later in the first chapter, after creating man in His image, we find the words, "God blessed them and said to them…" (Gen. 1:28). Here God gives a blessing along with words of instruction—specifically for mankind to populate and rule the earth. The final words in Genesis 1, which includes today's verses, reveal the wonderful nature of God as our Provider. He says, "I give…" and goes on to describe how the earth is ordained to meet our needs. The harvest of the land will be yours "for food," and it will also produce enough to feed the animals. Food, then, is a blessing, given to us by our heavenly Father, whose very nature is to meet our needs even before we recognize we have any.

In Psalm 136, a beautiful psalm of thanksgiving, the writer describes the enduring love of God toward us. It begins with an acknowledgment of God as the Creator of the universe (vv. 1–9), then speaks of Him as the One who is able to deliver us from the hand of our enemies (vv. 10–22), and concludes in recognition of His provisions:

> To the One who remembered us in our low estate
>> His love endures forever.
> And freed us from our enemies,
>> His love endures forever.
> And who gives food to every creature.
>> His love endures forever.
> Give thanks to the God of heaven.
>> His love endures forever.
>> —Psalm 136:23–26

One of the names of God is Jehovah-Jireh. Its Hebrew meaning reflects the generous attribute of God as a loving provider. In Genesis 22, God tested Abraham by calling him to sacrifice his son Isaac on Mount Moriah. Abraham obeyed God by taking Isaac to the mountain, binding him to the altar, and even lifting the knife to slay him. Just as he was prepared to bring the knife down on his son, God stopped him and provided an animal for him to sacrifice instead:

> Abraham looked up and there in a thicket he saw a ram caught
> by its horns. He went over and took the ram and sacrificed it

as a burnt offering instead of his son. So Abraham called that place The LORD Will Provide.

—Genesis 22:13–14

Abraham learned to know the goodness of God in a new way that day as a faithful provider to those who obey His commands. As we have seen, this same nature of God as Jehovah-Jireh was being manifested at the time of Creation. God, who met our need for food *before* creating us, also provided for Abraham, *before* Abraham recognized a need. I like to consider this sacrificial ram and how God determined that his destiny and purpose was to serve Abraham and Abraham's posterity long before the first step was taken on the journey to Mount Moriah.

King David declared the goodness of God as the One who meets our need for food in Psalm 37:

I was young and now I am old, yet I have never seen the righteous forsaken or their children begging bread.

—Psalm 37:25

Even Jesus, in the model prayer He taught His disciples, included the appeal to "give us today our daily bread" (Matt. 6:11). When we pray in this way, we are acknowledging that it is God in His goodness, and God alone, who sustains us. We trust Him each day to supply us with the things we need in order to survive, and we admit that we are incapable of meeting those needs by ourselves.

From the dawn of Creation, God has consistently shown Himself to be the One who meets our every need, including our need for food. During the wilderness experience, God sent miraculous food from heaven in the form of manna. Equally miraculous is how He has ordained for seed, soil, water, and sunlight to come together and yield a harvest of plenty.

The bountiful earth provides us with foods in a wide variety of tastes and textures for our enjoyment. God established that the fruit of the earth would nourish us, sustain us, and even protect us from diseases. Beyond our physical needs, food enhances fellowship and strengthens family ties. Appreciate food for what it is, a wonderful blessing from our wonderful God.

Daily Prayer

Father, may I never take Your blessings for granted but always acknowledge You as Jehovah-Jireh. I graciously accept Your provision of food for the blessing You intended it to be. Please guard my heart against the tendency to pervert this blessing by using food to meet any need outside of Your purpose and plan.

HEALTH FACT OF THE DAY
DAY FOUR

Approximately 30 percent of obese patients seeking weight-control treatment meet the psychiatric criteria for binge-eating disorder, a serious eating disorder in which one frequently consumes unusually large amounts of food.[1]

THE GOD OF POWER AND AUTHORITY

He got up, rebuked the wind and said to the waves, "Quiet! Be still!"
Then the wind died down and it was completely calm. He said to his
disciples, "Why are you so afraid? Do you still have no faith?" They were
terrified and asked each other, "Who is this? Even the wind and the
waves obey him!"

—MARK 4:39–41

GOD HAS POWER and authority over all. The triune God is a spirit, but we know from Scripture that "when the time had fully come, God sent his Son, born of a woman, born under law, to redeem those under law, that we might receive the full rights of sons" (Gal. 4:4–5).

In other words, Jesus (God the Son) took on human flesh for a period of time to accomplish the work of redemption for us. In very simplistic terms, human flesh was necessary because atonement required bloodshed, and spirits don't bleed.

But taking on humanity did not mean He relinquished His identity as God. During His earthly ministry, Jesus Christ was fully God and fully man. In our passage today from the Gospel of Mark, we see Him manifest power and authority over nature and perform a miracle that astonished His disciples.

Believers are indwelt by the Holy Spirit, who enables us to live in a manner that bears witness to our status as children of God. Paul, in his Epistle to the Colossians, makes this plain: "As you have therefore received Christ, [even] Jesus the Lord, [so] walk (regulate your lives and conduct yourselves) in union with and conformity to Him" (Col. 2:6, AMP).

How do we do this? Through our total reliance on the power and authority of God the Father, who blesses all who have faith in Jesus Christ with the indwelling of the Holy Spirit. By ourselves, we are powerless; through Christ, we are powerful. Consider the following verses:

So I say, *live by the Spirit*, and you will not gratify the desires
of the sinful nature.

—Galatians 5:16, emphasis added

Finally, be strong *in the Lord* and in his mighty power.

—Ephesians 6:10, emphasis added

I can do everything *through him* who gives me strength.

—Philippians 4:13, emphasis added

The unmistakable truth is that we, as believers, should live depend-
ently, not independently. Dependence on the Spirit leads to victory;
independence leads to defeat. But even though Scripture is plain about
who our source of power is, something has apparently gone amiss in our
understanding, our application, or both. I have observed innumerable
Christians professing they have God's power and proclaiming to operate
with Holy Ghost authority. But when I look for evidence of this in their
daily living, I find discrepancies such as:

- No power when it comes to making a decision as simple
  as choosing to drink water instead of a high-calorie
  beverage
- No authority over a choice as mundane as taking the
  stairs rather than the elevator
- No strength to definitively decide to maintain healthy
  habits and break unhealthy ones

This misconception of power is precisely why we, as Christians, are
suffering with more obesity and weight-related illnesses than any other
religious group. The multitudes of unbelievers we encounter each day
must surely be confused by the inconsistency between our words and our
actions. Indeed, they'd be justified in doubting whether the power we are
so quick to profess even exists.

Why are we not manifesting any power in our daily lives? I've come
up with three issues pertaining to weight control; most certainly there are
more, but let's examine these three:

1. We lack humility.

Many make the mistake of approaching weight loss and lifestyle modification armed with sheer will-power and self-determination. Even though they have committed Philippians 4:13 to memory, the emphasis and enthusiasm is directed toward "I can do everything." Unfortunately, the part of the verse that says "through him who gives me strength" becomes little more than an afterthought. But unless the priority is reversed, where we emphasize "Him" more than we emphasize what it is we want to accomplish, then success is not likely.

The apostle Paul gives us a good example of how humility is a prerequisite for power. In 2 Corinthians 12, after describing his thorn in the flesh, he said, "Therefore I will boast all the more gladly about my weaknesses, so that Christ's power may rest on me" (2 Cor. 12:9). Honestly admit to yourself that you have no power on your own to make the permanent lifestyle changes necessary for weight loss and better health. And then, according to James 4:6, God will grant you grace.

2. We are not vigilant.

Jesus said, "The thief comes only to steal and kill and destroy" (John 10:10). Peter said, "Be self-controlled and alert. Your enemy the devil prowls around like a roaring lion looking for someone to devour" (1 Pet. 5:8). John said, "When he [the devil] lies, he speaks his native language, for he is a liar and the father of lies" (John 8:44).

We cannot minimize the reality that Satan's purpose is to annihilate us. Yes, he does this through food temptation, but we must also recognize that he is a master of lies. One lie he has effectively conveyed to us is that gluttony is a laughing matter. Just notice how people giggle when talking about excessive eating. Or they will chuckle at the excuse they give for taking a second (or third) helping of food.

Don't get me wrong, I have a wonderful sense of humor, and I love to laugh. But I don't find anything funny about digging your own grave one forkful at a time. There is no humor in the disease and disability we bring upon ourselves through our eating habits. If you think it's funny, then I submit you have fallen for the deception planted by the father of lies. We can't experience the Lord's power until we first reject the devil's schemes.

3. We lack obedience.

"Do not merely listen to the word, and so deceive yourselves. Do what it says" (James 1:22). Sincere obedience to God's Word is the expectation for believers. Our motivation for persistent obedience is our love for the Lord, who then equips us to do what He has commanded. God's precepts concerning discipline, moderation, and self-control are vitally important for weight loss—you won't experience victory without them. The blessing is that He has equipped us to live them out by the power of the Holy Spirit.

Daily Prayer

Father, I acknowledge You as the sovereign Lord of heaven and Earth with authority and power over all creation. I thank You, Lord, for Your saving grace and Your indwelling Spirit. I humbly submit to You and thank You for giving me the power to lead a lifestyle that is edifying to my body and not destructive.

HEALTH FACT OF THE DAY
DAY FIVE

Regular use of a pedometer to monitor steps walked per day is associated with a significant increase in the level of physical activity and a significant decrease in the BMI and blood pressure.[1]

THE GOD OF SECOND CHANCES

If the LORD *delights in a man's way, he makes his steps firm; though he stumble, he will not fall, for the* LORD *upholds him with his hand.*

—PSALM 37:23–24

GOD ALONE IS perfect. We His children strive for perfection, and we miss the mark—on a regular basis! God, however, with mercy and compassion, does not turn His back on us when we fail. He gives us a second chance. Repentance always brings forgiveness. He is eternally gracious.

The goal for this fifty-day renewal is to become wholeheartedly committed to manifesting such biblical attributes as discipline, moderation, self-denial, and self-control in our everyday living. The expected *outcome* of this commitment is better health and the prevention or delay of diseases that are influenced by body weight, diet, and exercise. I think it is imperative that we keep the *goal* and the *outcome* distinct. A lifestyle of obedience to God's precepts is what our goal is. The outcome of weight loss is really just a bonus.

It seems this goal has eluded us because we have not fully grasped how vitally important it is to reject the ways of the world, to consistently resist temptation, and to recognize that the life of the believer is one of self-denial and not self-centeredness. We miss the mark, and our health suffers the consequences. But thank God for second chances.

Second chances reflect God's grace, a gift He freely grants to us. This is where we must be careful. It is possible to become so comfortable with this "grace guarantee" that we walk in error. We can misunderstand the concepts of liberty and grace and fall into the habit of deliberately yielding to the flesh simply because we know God will forgive us. But this is not how we should live. Let me illustrate this point with an example.

Have you ever been to the circus and seen a tightrope performance? The acrobats walk with extreme care. Even those with years of experience, those who are "mature" so to speak, still walk circumspectly. They diligently prepare themselves and practice regularly. They are confident

41

yet cautious. They are not hasty, but every movement is deliberate. They don't operate off the cuff, but are purposeful in their actions. Those who are excellent in their performance have certainly made mistakes, and the past mistakes become learning tools in their quest for perfection.

What I have never seen is a tightrope walker who is intentionally careless, unless he happens to be a clown. A serious acrobat does not take for granted what is required to stay on the rope. And they don't become lackadaisical about their performance just because there happens to be a safety net. I don't think any committed acrobat has a desire to end up in the net. When they do fall, it is not their *objective*; it is a *mistake*. Because it is an error, there comes with it a measure of embarrassment and shame. They may smile for the crowd, but they are not smiling on the inside. They don't dismiss it, they don't minimize it, and they resolve to proceed more carefully the next time.

By the same token, their shame does not overwhelm them or paralyze them. They are not sidelined because of their mistake. Being in the net humbles them and teaches them, but landing in the net does not deny them the opportunity of getting back on the rope. With mistakes come second chances.

The body of Christ could certainly learn a few things from circus performers! Yes, God has graciously secured us with a safety net so that when we make mistakes, we are not destined for eternal destruction. He is a God whose nature is mercy and compassion. He graciously forgives us. But our utmost desire should be to *stay on the rope*! Though the net is there, we should not set out to fall into it.

Self-denial and self-control will keep us on the rope. Self-indulgence and self-centeredness will find us in the net. Those desiring to reveal the nature of Christ in their daily walk and those who seek to obey God and glorify Him set out with a plan to stay on the rope. They accomplish this through the power of Jesus Christ. Our daily verse tells us when our ways delight the Lord, then He will make our steps firm. So God gives us the fortitude and stability required to live according to His precepts when we make the commitment to do so.

Clowns keep falling. Clowns even set out to fall. Clowns are good for a laugh, but they are ill-equipped for advancing the kingdom of God—something all believers are commissioned to do.

The apostle Paul spoke to this in his letter to the Romans: "What then? Shall we sin because we are not under law but under grace? By no means!" (Rom. 6:15). God's grace does not give license to cast off restraint. Paul goes on in the same chapter to describe how we are no longer slaves to our sin nature, but rather, we are slaves to obedience and righteousness. If, however, we make a deliberate choice to gratify the flesh nature, then we deny the liberating power of Jesus Christ. We then walk into bondage when we've been set free.

It is not enough to profess that God is our Lord and Master. We must also do His will. What we must guard against is the tendency to reject His precepts while choosing to take advantage of the "safety net" of forgiveness. Our loving Father's nature is that of patience, kindness, grace—and second chances. But God forbid we take these things for granted!

Daily Prayer

Dear Lord, I thank You for the promise never to leave me or forsake me. I thank You that You uphold me with Your hand when my ways are pleasing to You. I ask that You guard my heart against the tendency to take Your grace for granted. I am thankful for second chances, but don't allow me to use Your grace as a license to sin.

HEALTH FACT OF THE DAY

DAY SIX

Research done by the Diabetes Prevention Program Research Group showed that both lifestyle changes and treatment with the medication metformin both reduced the incidence of diabetes in persons at high risk for the disease. However, lifestyle intervention proved to be more effective than metformin.[1]

THE GOD OF WISDOM

Jesus called the crowd to him and said, "Listen and understand. What goes into a man's mouth does not make him 'unclean,' but what comes out of his mouth, that is what makes him 'unclean.'"

—MATTHEW 15:10–11

FIRST CORINTHIANS 14:33 says, "God is not the author of confusion" (KJV). So if food is provided by God, and God is not out to confuse us, then why is there so much uncertainty over what we should or should not eat?

A basic understanding of the way we ought to eat does not require an advanced degree in biochemistry or physiology. If we use godly wisdom and simply examine the "fearful and wonderful" way that God has created us, we can gain some understanding of what types of foods are most appropriate for us.

Since eating starts in the mouth, it makes sense to examine the way that God designed our teeth. Humans have relatively few sharp teeth—we have more flat molars than we do pointy canines. God created us with a predominance of flat teeth useful for grinding, with fewer sharp teeth that are needed for tearing meat. Unlike the carnivorous lions and tigers, whose teeth are ideally suited for ripping into flesh, most of our teeth are designed for grinding plants—grains, legumes, fruits, and vegetables.

It should come as no surprise, then, to find that our bowel habits are more regular when we consume a high-fiber diet composed primarily of plant-derived foods. Constipation is rarely a problem for people who eat plenty of fruits, vegetables, legumes, and whole grains. But the benefits of a high-fiber diet extend beyond bowel regularity.

It has been shown that diets with a low-fiber content increase the risk for type 2 diabetes and that increasing the consumption of dietary fiber (especially soluble fiber) will improve the blood sugar and lower the cholesterol and triglyceride levels in people with diabetes. And since God gave us teeth that are better suited for foods containing fiber, we shouldn't be surprised to learn that certain diet related illnesses such as cardiovascular disease and various forms of cancer are more common in people who eat an excessive amount of meat relative to plant-derived foods.

Godly wisdom requires us to restrict our diets to foods that promote good health. God implemented dietary guidelines even as far back as the Garden of Eden when He told Adam, "You are free to eat from any tree in the garden; but you must not eat from the tree of the knowledge of good and evil..." (Gen. 2:16–17). Dietary restriction is not punishment. God, in His wisdom, places limitations on us to protect us from harm. Clearly, once Adam and Eve violated their restrictions, harm soon followed.

Now let's consider the matter of eating meat. Before the Fall, God instructed Adam that mankind and animals were to live off the plants of the earth. Man and beast ate freely from every plant in the garden, including the fruit of the tree of life, which gave eternal life. Prior to the Fall, there was no death. As such, the very concept of killing for the purpose of food did not exist since both mankind and animals experienced eternal life.

The diet in the Garden of Eden was in keeping with this state of eternal life—there were no carnivores because there was no bloodshed. Vegetarianism was the first diet prescribed by God, and this type of diet can provide all the nutrients required for life. But we mustn't assume that it is a "better" way to eat because it was the first diet. Even angels eat meat. (See Genesis 18:1–8.)

When death entered the world, the original state of man—specifically man's relationship to animals—was altered. Animal skin became acceptable for clothing and animal flesh for food. This is confirmed in the covenant God established with Noah after the Flood. He told Noah and his family, "Everything that lives and moves will be food for you. Just as I gave you the green plants, I now give you everything" (Gen. 9:3). God permitted animals to be eaten as part of a covenant of *blessing* to man—eating meat is not "wrong."

A carnivorous diet does, however, require that we exercise more care and follow certain precautions to avoid consuming harmful bacteria and parasites. Unlike fruits and vegetables that can be eaten raw once properly washed, undercooked or contaminated meat, poultry, and fish can lead to a variety of illnesses, some even life threatening. We must also understand that meat should comprise a much smaller portion of our diets compared to plant-based food. Just because meat is OK doesn't mean it should dominate the plate.

Many generations after Noah came Moses and the Law. The nation of Israel was to remain separate because Jesus, the Messiah, was to be born of them. The Law served to preserve this race through its beneficial restrictions. The restrictions promoted health, they limited the spread of disease, and they served to maintain justice and civil order among the people.

Jesus fulfilled the Mosaic Law. We now live in a state of grace through faith in Christ and are no longer bound by legalism. But despite this liberty, far too many Christians are legalistic about their diets.

Don't misunderstand me—there is nothing wrong with controlling our appetites and limiting (or even eliminating) certain foods from our diets. In doing so, we keep our flesh under subjection. But while some level of dietary restraint is beneficial, too often we subject ourselves to unreasonable and unnecessary rules. Our eating habits become a form of legalism and can even lead to self-righteousness.

In their natural state, there really are no "acceptable" and "unacceptable" foods derived from God's bountiful earth. Of course, I must qualify this statement by the assumption that the food is suitable for human consumption, is fresh, unpolluted, and has not been harmfully processed or tampered with.

All food should be eaten in moderation, and some foods should be limited or even eliminated from the diet for medical reasons or for weight control. This does not make the food "bad"; it simply means that it is not beneficial for selected individuals with specific problems. It is up to us to use wisdom. We must keep food in its proper perspective and not pervert the blessing.

Jesus gives us profound wisdom in today's verse. What comes out of our mouths reflects what's inside our hearts. If the wisdom of God is there, we will be conscientious in the way we eat so that food nourishes our bodies and does not destroy them.

Daily Prayer

Lord, I ask for Your perfect wisdom to guide me in the foods I select and the quantities I eat. Help me to discern dietary truths from misleading fads. Help me to rely on wisdom rather than persuasive advertising in determining what I will and will not eat.

HEALTH FACT OF THE DAY
. DAY SEVEN

A large data analysis showed the key obesity drugs available in the United States have only a modest effect on weight loss. Orlistat reduced weight by approximately 6.4 pounds, and sibutramine by approximately 9 pounds.[1]

WEEKLY ASSESSMENT

My weight:	My BMI:	My waist size in inches:

I upheld my covenant by:

(Use a pencil and shade in the boxes starting from left to right to show how well you upheld your covenant this week.)

Less than 25%	25–49%	50–74%	75–99%	100%

VICTORIES: _____

_____

_____

_____

_____

_____

_____

PITFALLS: _____

_____

_____

_____

_____

_____

_____

WEEK TWO

Love Yourself

DAY **EIGHT**

EDIFICATION OR DESTRUCTION

For I am convinced that neither death nor life, neither angels nor demons, neither the present nor the future, nor any powers, neither height nor depth, nor anything else in all creation, will be able to separate us from the love of God that is in Christ Jesus our Lord.

—ROMANS 8:38–39

WE STARTED WEEK one by reviewing some of the attributes of God, which helps establish a foundation for our biblical approach to weight control. During this second week, we will examine our attitudes about ourselves. Without the proper attitude, we will not be equipped to make permanent changes to improve our health.

I believe the first order of business is to clarify our goals. Our primary goal is to optimize our health and to do what is within our control to minimize our risk for disease and disability. Our approach is through weight loss, however, I would expect that any destructive habit impacting your health will be subjected to the same biblical precepts we will cover for weight loss. Destructive habits such as excessive alcohol use, tobacco use, illegal drugs, sexual promiscuity, and even such things as a chronically stressful lifestyle and sleep deprivation should all be dealt with as we strive to reach the goal of optimal health.

So, we are embarking on this journey of spiritual renewal anticipating that by the end of our journey, through our obedience to the precepts of God and our yielding to the Holy Spirit, we will successfully implement a lifestyle that is edifying and not destructive to our physical bodies. The key concept here is "optimize." I believe God desires that we do all we can to preserve, maintain, and improve our health. But what we cannot take for granted is the reality that we live in a world tarnished by sin.

With the fall of mankind in the Garden of Eden, sin entered the world, and with it came disease, destruction, and death. One of the consequences of the Fall is that physical death (barring two notable exceptions) became our destiny. The two exceptions are found in the biblical accounts of translation whereby both Enoch and Elijah went straight to heaven, bypassing the dying process. (See Genesis 5:24; 2 Kings 2:11.) The Bible gives no further accounts of translation and makes no promise that anyone else should expect to get to heaven in this manner.

So, with the exception of these two men, along with every believer who will be yet living when Jesus returns, the rest of us have been given an appointment with death. This truth is confirmed in Scripture: "Just as *man is destined to die once,* and after that to face judgment, so Christ was sacrificed once to take away the sins of many people" (Heb. 9:27–28, emphasis added).

For the overwhelming majority of people, this appointment is met through disease. Certainly many people in perfect health die from tragic accidents, natural disasters, as victims of crime, or as casualties of war. But such deaths represent a small fraction of the total. Nearly every one of us will die from disease.

By now, you're probably wondering what such morbid talk has to do with your wanting to lose a few pounds and inches. I am making the point to clarify our goal of *optimizing* our health. We *cannot* set a goal of being *exempt* from all disease. This is not possible, and it is not biblical. But we *can* set a goal to do all we can to lower our risk of disease, to delay its onset, or to control it in the best possible manner should we find ourselves afflicted despite adhering to a healthy lifestyle.

Through my years of medical practice, I have met far too many Christians who believe that chronic diseases should not (or will not) come upon them because they have faith in Jesus Christ and are indwelt by the Holy Spirit. Oftentimes, when I diagnose disease, they challenge me as to whether or not I have faith in God's power to heal.

I've had men and women tell me they "do not receive" a diagnosis that has been established by such purely objective parameters as blood tests. So they ignore (or deny) the reality when the criteria used to diagnose disease aren't based on theology.

Suffice it to say, I have disappointed many Christian patients who assume I can bypass standard therapy, and instead rid them of any physical malady by speaking to their disease, laying hands on them, or simply believing that they are free of illness. And while I do pray for and with my patients on a regular basis, to dismiss evidence of disease (or not "receive" it) would be a tremendous disservice to these brothers and sisters.

What I find interesting is that more often than not, the same Christians who will not "claim" illness, are resistant to make lifestyle changes that will optimize their health. So an intriguing paradox evolves: there is an adamant refusal to make diet and exercise changes that will reduce the risk for developing disease and an equally adamant refusal to acknowledge the diseases that develop as a result of improper diet and inadequate exercise. As my daughter used to say, "Go figure!"

So our basic goal is to edify our bodies and not destroy them. This seems to be a simple concept when you read it in black and white, but statistics confirm this is easier said (or read) than done. Most of us miss the mark to some degree; certainly some more than others. The high prevalence of lifestyle-related illness—from diet- and exercise-related conditions to the many health consequences of smoking, alcohol, and drug use—bear witness to this truth.

In this week that we devote to loving ourselves, I hope to make the point that love will enable us to maintain our resolve to edify our bodies, and it will likewise help us to overcome those strong, persistent influences that persuade us to destroy them. Understand that we are constantly tempted by things that are destructive, and this temptation comes from a variety of sources: the world system, the devil, and even our flesh nature. But when we love ourselves in a biblical manner, we can prevail against all temptation.

In our daily verse, the apostle Paul emphasizes that nothing can separate us from the love of Christ, who has made us "more than conquerors through him who loved us" (Rom. 8:37). Let's make it a practice to live in a way that edifies our bodies, His temple, and experience victory in our health!

Daily Prayer

Lord, I thank You for equipping me with all that I need in order to take control of my lifestyle and improve my health. I am now able to resist the devil and subject my flesh through the power of the Holy Spirit. I embrace Your love for me and choose to love myself so that my lifestyle becomes one that is edifying, not destructive.

HEALTH FACT OF THE DAY
DAY **EIGHT**
Eating plenty of dark green leafy vegetables may reduce the risk of developing cataracts. Remember, overcooking fruits and vegetables will destroy some of their vitamins.

WHAT TRUE LOVE IS

And we have come to know and have believed the love which God has for us. God is love, and the one who abides in love abides in God, and God abides in him.

—1 JOHN 4:16, NAS

I F I MADE a list of personal grievances I have with the English language, the many uses (and abuses) of the word *love* would be close to the top of the list. Why is it that the same word that describes the profoundly intimate feeling a mother has for her child seems just as appropriate to use when describing our feeling for a piece of furniture, a style of clothing, or even a place like New York City? A clarification of terms is necessary for us to grasp the significance of love as defined for us by God.

The Greek language from which the New Testament was translated uses several different words to describe love. These words were applied appropriately for the conditions of love to which they referred.

For example, the Greek word *agape* describes love that is unconditional—*agape* is the essence of the Christian faith. It was this *agape* love of God for man that motivated Him to sacrifice His Son to restore His relationship with us. *Agape* love fulfills God's commandment to love our neighbors as ourselves (Matt. 19:19). It seeks the highest good for the recipient, even if he or she seems unworthy or even unappealing.

Agape is the love involving choice; we love unconditionally because we *will* to love. *Agape* love is not governed by our natural inclinations. It must at times ignore our natural emotional responses, choosing to love in spite of them. This is the love that covers all wrongs (Prov. 10:12).

The Greek word for the "touchy-feely" kind of love is *phileo*. It refers to tender affection—that warmth and compassion we have toward the object of our love. The feeling experienced between good friends is typical *phileo* love. The recipient makes the giver feel good. This positive feedback then becomes the driving force that generates more *phileo* love.

Though *agape* and *phileo* love can coexist, we need to understand their essential differences. A healthy marriage or a normal parent-child relationship should manifest both *agape* love and *phileo* love. There should be an unconditional acceptance in the relationship along with the "touchy-feely" response of *phileo*.

Unfortunately, it is *phileo* love that usually defines love for us. This fact has been a source of confusion, especially among new believers, when they learn that as Christians we are commanded to love our enemies (Matt. 5:44). That seems difficult (if not impossible) to do if we are relating to the "touchy-feely" conditions of *phileo* love. How can we love our enemy the way we love a relative or a close friend? How can we feel *phileo* love—tenderness, warmth, and affection—toward a person who has violated us and seeks to harm us?

Jesus never commanded us to love with *phileo* love. Instead, He asks that we love our enemies with *agape* love—the love that is based on a choice, not a feeling; the love that transcends the undesirable traits of the recipient; love that is unconditional. Of course, as we have mentioned, the source of *agape* love is God. He came to give His love to us and make it possible for us to experience unconditional love—for ourselves and others.

When a rich young man came to Jesus inquiring about spiritual matters, Jesus told him, "Do not murder, do not commit adultery, do not steal, do not give false testimony, honor your father and mother, and love your neighbor as yourself" (Matt. 19:18–19). It is rightly inferred from these commands that we must properly love ourselves, which in turn teaches us how to love our neighbor. And the word Jesus used for "love" in this command is *agape*—unconditional love based on choice.

Love ourselves. Right now. Just as we are. This is easier said than done because we live in a society that places extreme value on external appearances. The thin physique is idolized. You won't find many people striving to become overweight, but billions of dollars are spent each year on the quest to be thin. Social acceptance is often contingent upon the number on the scale. So if the prevailing attitude about obesity is negative, how is love possible?

Not only is it possible, but it is also a key to success. Loving yourself cannot be deferred until such time that you are pleased with your weight. That is why it is crucial to understand the distinction between *agape* and *phileo* love. Choosing to love ourselves as God loves us, regardless of our physical appearance, is a correct application of *agape* love. It is a choice; it is unconditional; it is a biblical command.

In contrast, *phileo* self-love is unhealthy. It is at the root of such vices as haughtiness, selfishness, and narcissism.

Agape self-love reflects God's acceptance of us. We are created in the image of God, and according to the Scriptures, God is love (1 John 4:8). It is logical, then, since we are created in the image of God, who loves us unconditionally, that we should love ourselves. Also, it is impossible to fulfill Christ's command to love our neighbor as ourselves in the absence of godly self-love.

I am often intrigued (and grieved) by how we manifest self-love. So often it is *phileo* in nature. We are motivated by a desire to "feel good" about ourselves, so we focus on self-adornment. The hair, make-up, clothing, and nails get a lion's share of our time, money, and attention. We visit the shopping mall, the spa, and even the plastic surgeon because we want to "feel good" about ourselves. *Phileo* love is "feel-good" love. And many are driven to "feel good" about themselves on the outside because there is an emptiness, a deficit of *agape* love, on the inside. Some call this low self-esteem, but the root problem is low *agape* love.

Agape love is unconditional love motivated by choice. It is not swayed by the standards set by society; it does not require that we be satisfied with our physical condition or pleased with our appearance. When we love ourselves with *agape* love, we choose to seek the highest good for our body, mind, and spirit, the recipients of that love, regardless of the way we feel about our bodies.

Success in weight loss requires lifestyle changes—changes that are always beneficial but quite often dramatic. The motivation we need to implement these changes and the determination needed to stick with them require an unconditional love for the one who stands to benefit from the change. This is what *agape* self-love is all about. It empowers us to do what is best for our body, contrary to what our feelings may dictate. And it is the work of the Holy Spirit, who empowers us to love ourselves properly. Love is what compels us to reject a lifestyle of self-destructive habits and behaviors—no matter how "set in our ways" we happen to be—and instead choose a lifestyle for better health.

Daily Prayer

Gracious Father, I thank You for Your love toward me, and I pray for a greater understanding of the nature of Your love. I

ask that You manifest Your agape love through me, and help
me to make healthy lifestyle choices based on this love.

HEALTH FACT OF THE DAY
DAY NINE

A study involving African American women showed the risk of diabetes was reduced in women who ate a diet that was high in cereal fiber, and this was evident among both overweight women and those who were not overweight. Changes as simple as switching from white bread to whole-grain bread, or substituting bran cereal or oatmeal for low-fiber breakfast foods could provide a 10 percent reduction in diabetes risk.[1]

OUR BODIES, HIS TEMPLE

Do you not know that your body is a temple of the Holy Spirit, who is in you, whom you have received from God? You are not your own; you were bought at a price. Therefore honor God with your body.

—1 CORINTHIANS 6:19–20

IN OLD TESTAMENT times, the place for sacrifice was the temple. The act of sacrifice required a person to give up something of value that belonged to him. But why did God ordain this practice? Certainly, God did not *need* the sacrifice; the person presenting the offering was doing God no favor. What, then, was the purpose?

It was simply a way to tangibly express thankfulness to God for His goodness and His mercy, providing restitution as well for any offense committed against God. In other words, it was a way to express love. This sacrificial ritual, which was a basic form of worship, was performed daily.

From the start, the practice was subject to corruption because of religious hypocrites who turned it into a pointless ritual. But despite this tendency toward corruption, the Bible records for us lives of individuals who offered sincere and meaningful sacrifices that pleased God.

For example, God asked Abraham to sacrifice Isaac, his son. Abraham cherished Isaac; he was the long-awaited child promised to him by God. Yet, his willingness to sacrifice his son was proof of Abraham's unwavering faith, his obedience, and most importantly, his love for the Lord. God's poignant response to Abraham's obedience reveals how pleased He was by Abraham's love: "Now I know that you fear God, because you have not withheld from me your son, your only son" (Gen. 22:12).

Sacrifice is not exclusive to the Old Testament. Paul, in his Epistle to the Romans, wrote, "Therefore, I urge you, brothers, in view of God's mercy, to offer your bodies as living sacrifices, holy and pleasing to God—this is your spiritual act of worship" (Rom. 12:1). Sacrifice is still required, but our offering is no longer the nicest lamb in our flock. Instead, we symbolically place ourselves on the altar of the Lord. We are living sacrifices; we lay aside our own desires to embrace a higher purpose.

At Pentecost, the Holy Spirit came to dwell in believers. From today's verse, we know the temple of God is no longer a structure made of stone, but the Holy Spirit lives in us. If we love God, then we must express that love toward His temple, our bodies. We do that when we make a commitment to live a healthy lifestyle, even if it requires us to "sacrifice" something we enjoy. Popular diets have such an appeal because they promise the "gain" of weight loss without the "pain" of sacrifice. But the adage is true: no pain, no gain. Permanent weight loss only happens when there is a willingness to embrace sacrifice as a vital part of love.

The average person thinks of a "diet" in terms of temporary deprivation, not a lifestyle change. The result of that kind of thinking is a *goal-oriented* mind-set. The primary focus becomes the "end" of the diet, whether that happens to be next week, next month, or even next year. We promise ourselves, "If I can continue with this agony for just a little longer, I'll be able to fit into that dress." Our temporary deprivation has a goal to meet a specified end.

The worst part about this attitude is that along with anticipation of the end, there is also a plan for rewarding ourselves upon reaching the goal, usually with the very foods that were temporarily denied. From day one, we start to think about those reward foods—the cheesecake and the ice cream—that will be eaten with abandon once the goal is met. We set ourselves up to fail, and we pervert the neutral status of food. For habitual "dieters," food takes on the character of being "good" or "bad," a "reward" or a "punishment."

Permanent weight loss requires us to stop thinking in terms of temporary change. We don't need a "diet" that adjusts our menu for a week or two; we need a "diet" that will permanently change our attitude about food, our lifestyles, and the way we treat God's living temple. Our attitude must reflect a spirit of sacrificial love, which makes us willing to give up a few things we enjoy for the greater purpose of good health.

Keep in mind, changing our behavior to improve our health is a positive choice, even though it involves sacrifice. We need to overcome the tendency to view sacrifice in a negative light. Sacrifice is not penance, nor is it a form of torture. It should not be done begrudgingly but with an attitude of joyful thanksgiving. Sacrifice is a manifestation of love, and our attitude toward a healthy lifestyle should reflect that love.

Over the years, those patients in my practice who have been successful at losing weight have all come to terms with the inevitability of sacrifice. Their testimonies are never affirmations that losing weight was an easy thing to do. Instead, they confirm that success was dependent upon changing a behavior or eliminating a habit:

- "I learned to cook beans and lentils, and I often eat them in place of meat."
- "I used to buy a candy bar every day to eat on my way home, but I broke that habit."
- "Now I get out of bed a half-hour earlier to exercise on my treadmill."

It's all about sacrifice—a willingness to forgo something we might enjoy (whether meat, sweets, or an extra half-hour of sleep) for the higher purpose of better health.

Some things require a total sacrifice. For example, adults should replace whole milk with reduced-fat or skim milk. Other foods require a partial sacrifice. We don't have to totally eliminate them from our diet, but we should restrict them in terms of the frequency with which we eat them.

And this is the mind-set we must maintain for permanent weight loss. We have bought into the notion that losing weight should be easy, but unfortunately, this is not true. It requires sacrifice. Simply put, some of our habits must be placed on the altar and symbolically burned. They need to be sacrificed willingly out of love for God and a desire to do whatever it takes to guard His living temple against disease and illness.

John records that many of Jesus's disciples grumbled after hearing His revolutionary teaching. Jesus was saying that He was the Bread of Life and that we must eat that bread to live forever (John 6:51). They said to each other, "This is a hard teaching. Who can accept it?" (v. 60). Some did not accept it; they turned away and no longer followed Him. Their turning away did not change the validity of Jesus's teachings; it only demonstrated that even some of those who followed Jesus were not ready to accept the truth.

The call to live sacrificially is also a hard teaching, and not everyone will be able to accept it. The promoters of fad diets have convinced us that losing weight should be on our terms—easy and effortless. They have persuaded us so well that any suggestion to the contrary is not readily accepted.

But the truth of the matter is that losing weight requires that we change our lifestyles. And change, for most of us, does not come easily. What, then, will make us willing to change a lifestyle that is familiar to us? What will allow us to maintain a new way of living? Sacrificial love. If the Spirit of God is in us, we have that love as well as a powerful motivator to encourage us and equip us.

The fruit of the Spirit of love will help us to change our attitudes about our bodies. We are not merely bones and flesh; we are the living temples of God, and as such, we are of great value to God.

Once we embrace the truth that we are God's living temples, our love for God will empower us to make whatever sacrifices are required to keep our temples in optimal health. As we grow in the fruit of the Spirit of love, sacrifice becomes easier because our deepest desire will no longer be to please ourselves but to please God.

Daily Prayer

Father, I ask that You quicken in me the desire to worship You through a spirit of sacrifice. Help me to see this day that I am not my own but that You purchased me at a high price. Help me to honor You in all things, including the way I treat my body, Your temple.

HEALTH FACT OF THE DAY
DAY TEN

Studies consistently show an association between sleep apnea and hypertension that is independent of the effects of obesity on blood pressure. People with moderate sleep apnea have an almost threefold greater risk of developing hypertension than people without sleep apnea.[1]

DAY ELEVEN

MANAGING THE CLOCK AND MINIMIZING STRESS

"Martha, Martha," the Lord answered, "you are worried and upset about many things, but only one thing is needed. Mary has chosen what is better, and it will not be taken away from her."

—Luke 10:41–42

THERE NEVER SEEMS to be enough time to accomplish everything we need to do. Consequently, we let ourselves get pulled in several different directions, and rather than experiencing peace, we feel pressure.

In the past few decades, time management has taken on a new level of significance. There are seminars conducted specifically for this purpose, attended by hundreds of people, all seeking to become better managers of time. The sponsors first lay the groundwork by pointing out the many ways we waste time. Then they go on to suggest that the best way to preserve our valuable time is through using their highly sophisticated gadgets. Major corporations pay for their executives to attend these seminars, expecting their investment to pay off with increased productivity and increased revenue—all because of optimally managed time.

Americans are obsessed with time. We have convinced ourselves that we will be better off if we can just speed up. By learning to do whatever it is we do just a little bit faster, we can squeeze a few more activities into an already frantic day.

When we believe the twenty-four hours we've been allotted is simply not enough, we create stress for ourselves. Unfortunately, the typical response to this stress is not to remove items from our "things to do" list—which would be the most rational approach. Instead, we usually try to restructure our priorities in a way that allows more time for those things we feel are urgent and less time for everything else.

The things we perceive as being urgent are usually those things that give us an immediate sense of accomplishment. But some things are vitally important yet will not give us any quick rewards. Living a healthy

63

lifestyle is a good example of this. The benefits are long-term, not instant. The time we devote to our health, however, is prone to fall a notch or two down our list of priorities when we feel pressed for time.

For many, making the switch from an unhealthy diet to a healthy one requires a fair amount of time and effort. Learning new cooking methods, new recipes, and how to plan meals requires time—time that must be factored into an already tight schedule. When the demands are high and time is limited, the temptation to resort to the old, unhealthy way of eating is extremely powerful. This is when we're prone to eat out—a "quick" solution that can be harmful to our health.

When I ask my patients who are struggling to lose weight how often they eat out each week, I am stunned by the answers I receive. The reasons they give for eating out are invariably connected to their perception of time. They've determined they simply cannot spare the time necessary to prepare a healthy meal. So instead, they eat out for breakfast, lunch, or dinner, and sometimes all three.

There are now 925,000 restaurants in the United States, and we eat an average of one out of five meals outside the home. Clearly, this bears witness to the notion that avoiding the grocery store and the kitchen will "save time." Restaurant blueprints confirm our misconception. When fast-food restaurants were first developed, they were similar to full-service restaurants in that they provided plenty of indoor seating. Then the drive-through window came along, which gave us the option of getting the food without even stepping inside or turning off our engine. And now, some fast-food "restaurants" don't even have seats. They are designed with nothing but drive-through and walk-up service. Mealtime is relegated to the car, the bus, the taxi, or even as we walk down the street.

Our problem is not that we lack time. Time is a constant—twenty-four hours each day, no more, no less. So when we feel pressured by time constraints, it's not that time has grown scarce; it's that we are trying to fit too many activities into an unyielding and constant variable. The question is not, "What is the best way to manage my time?" Rather, it is, "What is the best way to structure my priorities?"

An example of maintaining the right priorities is found in the account of Mary and Martha in Luke 10. Martha thought she was right on target, but Jesus pointed out that it was Mary who was the better time manager because her priorities were set based on what was *important*, rather than what was *urgent*.

It is important that we recognize our tendency to respond like Martha to life's demands and then discipline ourselves to behave more like Mary. We need to make sure that long-term priorities have the right place in our lives. This is especially true for women, who have a greater presence in the workplace now compared to the past few generations but are still charged with maintaining the home and raising children. Even with the most supportive, involved husband and the highest quality child care, the challenge to meet the needs of both the workplace and the family is unrelenting. For the single parent, it can be overwhelming.

No matter how great the demands of life, it is crucial that we allow adequate time for the important things that may not have instantaneous results. Every Christian would agree that time should be set aside each day for prayer, meditation, and Bible study. The long-term benefit is spiritual growth and a closer walk with God. But since these activities may not generate as strong a sense of urgency as some of our other obligations, they are often neglected. We find ourselves rushing through a short psalm or speed-reading a page from a book of daily devotions, then concluding our "quality time with the Lord" with a quick, cursory prayer.

In the same way, the time we devote to our health will yield more long-term results than instant rewards. Consequently, it tends to receive a priority rank much lower than those things that give us an immediate sense of gratification or accomplishment. For those people who are obese or overweight or who have a medical condition that requires lifestyle modification, this is a serious mistake. Daily attention to our health will serve to prevent, delay, or reduce the complications of many diseases, including cardiovascular disease, diabetes, and cancer. Even people who have a normal body weight with no illnesses will reap long-term rewards by devoting sufficient time toward maintaining good health.

The time God gives us each day is not subject to change. But what we do with that time certainly is. The choice of how we use it is ours. Make the choice for better health.

Daily Prayer

Lord, grant me wisdom for how I spend the time You give me each day. Help me to set priorities that are beneficial to my health and the health of my family. Give me the patience and endurance I need to fulfill my long-term goals.

HEALTH FACT OF THE DAY

DAY ELEVEN

Children who share mealtime with their families eat more fruits and vegetables and do better in school than children who eat separately.[1]

TWENTY-FIRST-CENTURY IDOLATRY

You shall not make for yourself an idol in the form of anything
in heaven above or on the earth beneath or in the waters below.
You shall not bow down to them or worship them; for I,
the LORD *your God, am a jealous God.*

—EXODUS 20:4–5

THERE IS A tendency among Christians to let cultural differences bias our evaluation of some Old Testament passages of Scripture. It is appropriate to read the Bible with a consideration of such things as the era, the political structure, and the lifestyle of the people. This is crucial if we are seeking a clearer understanding of the Word of God. What we must guard against, however, is the tendency to think that the warnings in the Bible that seem foreign to us are only relevant to the time and culture in which they were written. This line of thinking is erroneous because God's Word is timeless. The verses for today give us a good example of how we must guard against this tendency.

Certainly, we don't see icons like golden calves and carved images in our sanctuaries today, but that does not nullify the second commandment. The tendency toward idolatry rests in the heart of man. The *things* he chooses to worship may vary depending on the period and the culture, but the *bent* toward idolatry transcends the passage of time and the modernization of society. That being the case, we'd be wise to examine this matter of idolatry as it relates to us in the twenty-first century. Our loving Father would not have given us the Ten Commandments if they were no longer applicable.

First, let's erase the impressions of molten gold and carved wood from our minds and consider the matter of idolatry, rather than the idol per se. The sin of idolatry occurs when we offer those things reserved *for* God to the things created *by* God. Our worship, for instance, is reserved for God. By "worship," I don't mean a Sunday-only event, and I don't mean only music and singing. I'm referring to a lifestyle marked by a passionate pursuit for Him.

Along with worship, we also grant God the authority to govern our behavior. This is manifested in a willingness to obey His precepts and submit to the way He has instructed us to live. We don't offer our opinion, and we don't make an analysis of God's expectation of us. We simply obey.

When something else assumes these roles in our lives—that is, when we passionately pursue something other than God or when we obediently submit to an authority that is not God Himself or God ordained, then we have slipped into the sin of idolatry. Of course, money and power are common idols in every era, including our own. It is not uncommon to see Christians, even those in leadership, pursuing money and power with more passion than they pursue righteousness. They allow the love of money and power to control their actions. The idols of money and power are destructive and often go unrecognized—even by those who profess spiritual discernment.

But there are other idols in our age that are wreaking havoc just like the idols of money and power, and I believe (while some may disagree) that addiction is one of these idols. There have been many Christians over the years who take offense to the idea that nicotine addiction, for instance, is detrimental to the physical *as well as* the spiritual health. Few people will challenge that there is physical harm. It is no longer speculated, but it is a proven fact that the substances introduced into the body from cigarette smoking cause disease, disability, and premature death. But these same Christians may not be ready to accept the concept of addiction as a spiritual matter, specifically that it should be considered a form of idolatry.

Keep in mind, however, that an idol is a thing created *by* God and we have given this thing the authority that should be reserved *for* God. If a substance like nicotine controls my behavior to the extent that I will use it despite the fact that it will place my health in serious jeopardy, then it has a power over me that is tantamount to idol worship. Likewise, if I need nicotine in order to feel peace and comfort, then I have allowed it to provide for me a counterfeit to the true peace and comfort that only God can give. No molten gold. No carved wood—but idolatry nonetheless.

Now, let's consider the matter of food. Food, as we have said, is a blessing from God. Food itself is neutral, as is gold and wood. But what we are prone to do with food and the place food occupies in our thoughts and hearts reveals if we have crossed the line from *appreciating* the blessing to *idolizing* the blessing. In order to tease out the sin of idolatry, we must be willing to be painfully honest and brutally introspective. Hebrews 4:12 tells us that the penetrating Word of God "judges the thoughts and attitudes of the heart." With this in mind, ask yourself the following questions:

1. How much time do I spend thinking about food and eating? How does that compare to the time I spend thinking about God?
2. Am I prone to lose control with eating? Do I have food cravings that are sometimes too strong to suppress?
3. How difficult is it for me to deny myself food for the purpose of a spiritual fast?
4. Do I use food to calm my nerves? To soothe any emotional wounds? To ease the pain of hurtful things like rejection and personal loss?
5. Do I feel the need to eat in secret? Do I feel embarrassed to the extent that I hide food from others in my household who might criticize my eating?

While tobacco, excessive alcohol, and illegal drugs are easily identified problems, food idolatry often goes unrecognized for several reasons. For starters, overeating is socially acceptable. While most of us are uncomfortable or even repulsed by being in the company of someone who is drunk with alcohol, the one who loses control with food and eats excessively goes completely unnoticed.

A second factor is that there is a dangerous sense of security in numbers. We are heavily tempted and constantly encouraged to eat more than we need, to the extent that overeating is now the norm. And when "everyone is doing it," it becomes easy to rationalize a behavior as acceptable when it is, in fact, unacceptable.

Finally, unlike tobacco, alcohol, and drugs, which can be completely eliminated from a person's life, we cannot eliminate food. Our goal is not to make food taboo but to stop the passionate pursuit of it and appreciate it as one of God's many blessings. While we are learning to change our attitude about food, we are obliged to regularly expose ourselves to our weakness, the very thing we are prone to idolize. The advice given to alcoholics is to totally abstain from all alcohol to avoid losing control, but survival precludes us from giving the same advice to overeaters.

God has given us a timeless warning to guard ourselves against the sin of idolatry. It is interesting that in describing Israel's turning away, God said, "Jeshurun grew fat and kicked; filled with food, he became heavy and sleek. He abandoned the God who made him and rejected the Rock his Savior" (Deut. 32:15). Don't overlook what might be an idol in your life. If food meets the criteria, then turn to God's Word and pray fervently. Position yourself for deliverance, and God will provide it.

Daily Prayer

Lord, I thank You for opening my eyes to the sin of idolatry. I ask that You remove any hindering spirit of pride that denies the potential for idol worship in my life and during this present age. I thank You for being my firm foundation, my strong tower, and a very present help in time of trouble.

HEALTH FACT OF THE DAY

DAY TWELVE

A 2005 study in the *New England Journal of Medicine* suggests that life expectancy at birth and at older ages could level off or even decline within the first half of the twenty-first century as a result of the substantial rise in the prevalence of obesity and its life-shortening complications such as diabetes.[1]

MADE TO MOVE

She sets about her work vigorously; her arms are strong for her tasks.
—PROVERBS 31:17

GOD DESIGNED OUR bodies to be physically active. We were made for movement. This is confirmed when we consider the diseases associated with a sedentary lifestyle in contrast to the health benefits gained through exercise. Exercise protects against cardiovascular disease (hypertension, stroke, and heart disease), reduces the risk for some forms of cancer, and lowers the odds for developing diabetes. Exercise also strengthens the bones, improves the mood, preserves our cognitive function, gives us a better night's sleep, and plays a fundamental role in weight loss. Research confirms that regular exercise prolongs life and reduces the burden of disability and disease as we grow older.

Despite the proven benefits, most of us are not exercising. Only 30 percent of adults engage in regular, leisure-time physical activity, and 39 percent engage in no leisure-time activity at all. The term "leisure time" refers to time set aside for the purpose of physical activity.

Advances in technology have changed the way we live. Where we once were physically active by default (that is, we earned a living and kept our homes by the literal sweat of our brow), our culture now has afforded us the option of being "couch potatoes." But we don't have to choose that option. In fact, God's desire is that we reject it. Certainly we won't find in Scripture the command, "Thou shalt exercise regularly," but we definitely have an example in the Book of Proverbs that speaks toward an active lifestyle.

Proverbs 31 gives a description of the wife of noble character, a woman of wisdom with virtues all of us should strive to achieve. She is a first-class wife and mother who maintains her home well. She is generous and business minded. Her managerial skills are excellent and so is her handiwork. She is not careless with her resources, nor is she slothful. She knows how to prioritize her time so that the day is never wasted. And, finally, "her arms are strong." She's in shape. Isn't it interesting that God thought

71

it necessary to include in the list of qualities we need to know—traits we should strive to emulate—the fact that she was physically fit.

There is nothing to suggest, either from the Proverbs 31 account or from an understanding of the culture, that this virtuous woman belonged to a gym or designated a specific time during the day for exercise. She wouldn't have had the privilege of being included among the 30 percent of adults in our time who engage in regular, leisure-time activity because it does not appear she had much leisure time. The Bible says, "She gets up while it is still dark" (v. 15) and "her lamp does not go out at night" (v. 18). And, based on the description of her life, the time in between was spent fulfilling her responsibilities, which could not be accomplished in a sedentary manner. She didn't shy away from exerting herself. To the contrary, we're told she approached her work "vigorously." Her lifestyle gave her plenty of exercise.

Many women are unsettled by the account of the Proverbs 31 wife. And now she has intimidated us on yet another level by destroying the "I don't have time to exercise" excuse. She didn't have time to exercise either. Nevertheless, her arms were strong. She was well conditioned, she was physically fit, and she never joined a health club. So even though many complain they have no extra time to devote to exercise, we, like the Proverbs 31 woman, can incorporate exercise into our lives even if we can't seem to find any leisure time. What we must do is make a concerted effort to move more. (As an aside, I honestly believe that modern technology has afforded us time we otherwise would not have at our disposal. If we model the Proverbs 31 woman's ability to *manage* time, I think we'd find we actually *do* have leisure time available to devote to exercise. It's all a matter of how we set our priorities.)

Staying active in a culture that promotes inactivity requires that we go against the grain. As Christians, however, going against the grain should be a standard to which we are accustomed: "Do not conform any longer to the pattern of this world, but be transformed by the renewing of your mind. Then you will be able to test and approve what God's will is—his good, pleasing and perfect will" (Rom. 12:2). Just as we reject the pattern of the world in the spiritual sense, we must likewise reject its pattern in the natural. And that pattern is one of physical inactivity. In *choosing* that pattern, we concurrently make the choice for disease, disability, and premature death. In *rejecting* that pattern, we honor God through protecting and preserving our bodies, His temple.

Any extra movement is good, but we must get into the habit of seeking out opportunities to move. One of my biggest pet peeves is watching people who are fully capable of walking drive around a parking lot, looking for a space close to the entrance. And real agitation sets in when I happen to get stuck behind that person as they wait for someone to pull out of a "nice" space. Chances are high that if they are overweight, they'd like to lose weight; and chances are high that if the parking lot is for a grocery store, at least one of the items purchased will be "low fat" or "low calorie" or some other product to facilitate weight loss; and chances are high that they believe they don't have time in their busy day to set aside for regular exercise. But then they drive up and down the aisle, forfeiting a great opportunity to increase their physical activity simply by choosing a parking place at a distance from the door.

I once practiced on the third floor of an ambulatory clinic building that was a state-of-the-art structure with glass-encased staircases and halls. Anyone climbing the stairs or walking the halls was visible from the street and even from various locations inside the building. I was always amazed at the fact that most of the times I looked at the stairway, it was empty. It hardly mattered what time of day or what day of the week, there was usually no one climbing or descending the stairs. I was amazed because I had personally advised literally hundreds of patients to increase their daily activity by using the stairs rather than the elevators, but I never saw anyone climb the stairs to get to my office. Another forfeited opportunity to move.

God designed our bodies in a way that our physical, mental, and emotional health is improved through movement. Become determined in your daily activities to take advantage of opportunities to move. Then scrutinize your daily routine and restructure your priorities so that you also make time for regular exercise.

Daily Prayer

Dear Lord, I repent for the tendency to neglect my health by ignoring the need to exercise. Help me to keep my commitment to move more in my daily activities, as well as set aside time in my day for exercise.

HEALTH FACT OF THE DAY

DAY THIRTEEN

The Harvard Alumni Study found that men who averaged at least eight flights of stairs a day had a 33 percent lower mortality rate than men who were sedentary.[1]

DAY **FOURTEEN**

CELEBRATE WITH FOOD

When the hour came, Jesus and his apostles reclined at the table.
And he said to them, "I have eagerly desired to eat this Passover with
you before I suffer. For I tell you, I will not eat it again until it finds
fulfillment in the kingdom of God."

—LUKE 22:14–16

ODAY MARKS THE end of week two, the week where we've focused on loving ourselves. On this day, I think it is appropriate to consider how our heavenly Father has blessed us with food, and how He has given us food not just to nourish and sustain us but also for the purpose of bringing His children together. Yes, we are to love Him, and we are to love ourselves, but we must also love one another. Food provides a wonderful means for establishing relationships among strangers and enhancing fellowship between friends and family.

Like any blessing, food can be perverted by the devil and our flesh nature to the extent that the blessing is used to curse. But it is vitally important that we recognize food in the manner God intended—for our nourishment, enjoyment, and to draw us closer to one another.

Believe it or not, I really enjoy eating, and I really enjoy good food. Yes, I avoid unhealthy foods, but I certainly appreciate good food. I am constantly meeting people who consider "good-tasting food" and "healthy food" to be contradictory terms, as if "tasty health food" is an oxymoron. This couldn't be further from the truth.

Not too long ago, I brought refreshments to a meeting we had at our church. After sampling some of my dishes, one of the newer members of the congregation came to me and confessed she felt much better about my husband, our pastor. She was under the impression that he suffered daily because I gave him nothing to eat other than healthy meals. She knew him to be a kind man and assumed he would never insult me but would silently endure with sacrificial love in accordance to Ephesians 5:22. After tasting the dishes I prepared, her comments were, "And this is healthy?" "You mean this is good for you?" I told her my husband was the biggest

75

fan of good-tasting food in our household, and I was a close second. To think you must compromise good taste in order to eat right is simply not true, and I was happy to dispel this myth for her.

Let's first look at some examples of how food is used for fellowship, and then I'll close the week with a few tips on how to celebrate using food in a God-honoring way.

Our daily verse gives the account of Jesus's last Passover celebration. The Passover and the Feast of Unleavened Bread are momentous holidays for Jewish people, marking their miraculous deliverance from Egyptian bondage. Food is always a part of the celebration, in fact, God Himself established the kinds of foods they were to eat and how they were to prepare them to properly commemorate the event.

The first of Jesus's miracles recorded in the Gospel of John took place at a wedding feast where Jesus turned water into wine. Food fellowship was integral to important life events, and Jesus chose to demonstrate His power and glory at one such celebration.

After the church was established at Pentecost, we are told the believers "devoted themselves to the apostles' teaching and to the fellowship, to the breaking of bread and to prayer" (Acts 2:42). Indeed, sharing a meal together was so vitally important to the early church that the Holy Spirit inspired Luke, the author, to mention it right along with teaching and prayer. Certainly, we should not underestimate the extent to which food is a blessing from God for our nourishment, enjoyment, and to promote unity and fellowship.

Our celebrations today would be uninspiring without a meal. I can't imagine observing Thanksgiving or Christmas without food. Even less significant events like birthdays, graduations, and anniversaries include food as an essential part of the celebration. During life's painful transitions—a serious illness or the death of a loved one—food is offered to those grieving as a tangible expression of love.

Yes, food is a blessing that God intends we use to seal relationships and express our love for one another. We glorify Him when we share a meal with our hearts on one accord. The blessing of food can be perverted by our flesh or used for our destruction by the devil, but let's not throw the baby out with the bathwater! Even if we are trying to lose weight or if we must restrict our diets because of a medical condition, we can't deny ourselves the opportunity to celebrate with food. What we must learn to do is stay cognizant of our tendency to turn a godly food fellowship into a gluttonous food orgy. Here are a few suggestions to help maintain the former and not slip into the latter:

1. **Celebrate at home.** One trend that has crept into our celebrations is that now, unlike in biblical times, we are likely to share a meal in a restaurant rather than in our homes. While this may be convenient in terms of eliminating the need to cook and clean, it does take away from the fellowship, and it predisposes us to eat too much of the wrong types of foods. Restaurant meals often have too much fat, too many calories, and an unacceptably high sodium content. The portions tend to be excessive, which presents a problem since we usually eat whatever is set before us. Outside of the food itself, eating out does not afford us the opportunity to show hospitality, a character trait God expects of believers. (See Romans 12:13; Hebrews 13:2; 1 Peter 4:9.)

2. **Use wisdom in planning your menu.** Try a spread made with beans instead of cream cheese; a whole-grain pasta primavera instead of a bacon quiche; a berry cobbler dessert instead of cheesecake. Then modify dishes that are family traditions so that they contain fewer calories, less saturated fat, and less sodium.

3. **Provide take-home containers in lieu of second servings.** How about motivating your guests to make lifestyle changes for better health along with you. Suggest they put what they would have eaten as seconds in a "to-go" container to enjoy for lunch the following day.

4. **Be careful with beverages.** Even if you serve a punch or carbonated beverages, be sure to also serve calorie-free or low-calorie beverages like water, coffee, and tea.

5. **Appreciate family and friends more than the food.** Remember, the primary purpose is fellowship, not engorgement. Keep that at the forefront of your mind, whether you are the host or a guest.

Daily Prayer

Lord, I give thanks for the blessing of food. Help me to use this blessing as a way to establish and maintain relationships, and

*even as a tool for reunion and reconciliation for those I have
fallen out of fellowship with. Please guard my heart against the
tendency of my flesh to pervert Your blessings and help me be
discerning so that I might see the devil's plan to destroy my
health through eating.*

HEALTH FACT OF THE DAY
DAY FOURTEEN

The average daily sodium intake in the United States
is about 4,000 mg of sodium for every 2,000 calories,
with the typical restaurant meal having between one and
two teaspoonfuls of salt. With intakes this high, the vast
majority of Americans can expect to develop high blood
pressure at some point during their lifetimes.[1]

WEEKLY ASSESSMENT

My weight:	My BMI:	My waist size in inches:

I upheld my covenant by:

(Use a pencil and shade in the boxes starting from left to right to show how well you upheld your covenant this week.)

Less than 25%	25–49%	50–74%	75–99%	100%

VICTORIES: _____

_____

_____

_____

_____

_____

_____

PITFALLS: _____

_____

_____

_____

_____

_____

_____

Maintaining the Right Attitude

DAY **FIFTEEN**

STAYING FOCUSED

For by the grace given me I say to every one of you: Do not think of yourself more highly than you ought, but rather think of yourself with sober judgment, in accordance with the measure of faith God has given you.

—ROMANS 12:3

W EEK THREE OF our fifty-day journey takes us on a little detour. We will devote this week to a different type of soul searching. Our primary focus will be learning how to turn our attention away from the subject of losing weight, per se, and focus on our attitude about food.

Now, before you skip on to week four, rest assured that I recognize that the most likely reason you are reading this is because you have struggled with obesity or you have a weight-related health problem. So, the last thing you may have expected during your reading is to encounter an entire segment that ignores the tangible ways to approach your problem. A full week devoted to something other than how to lose weight may not, at first glance, seem to have any bearing on your pursuit.

But I guarantee you that this temporary change in focus does not compromise my objective. To the contrary, I expect that you will find that the information gleaned during this week provides what had been the missing link in prior weight loss attempts. Our attitude about ourselves, others, and food itself is a major determinant of our success.

In today's verse, the apostle Paul speaks to "every one of you," which includes you and me, and identifies a trait common to us all. He reminds us of the tendency to focus too much of our attention on ourselves, and then he counsels us to correct this ungodly habit.

While we are prone to self-centered thinking at all times and in all circumstances, it becomes especially evident when we are confronted with a problem. When things aren't going our way, the characteristic response is to become totally absorbed by whatever troubles us. It doesn't matter what the problem happens to be—whether it involves our finances, our health, or our relationships—this total immersion is typical.

When we're in a trying situation, we don't limit ourselves to cursory thoughts. We systematically dissect every aspect of the problem, repeatedly analyzing every angle in an attempt to come to terms with the nagging question, "Why me?" when the apostle Paul's words should provoke us to ask, "Why *not* me?"

When we habitually think of ourselves more highly than we ought, it's not long before our personal issues and inconveniences occupy the forefront of our minds throughout the day. Though we try not to worry, we find ourselves preoccupied and even anxious until the time when the problem is resolved. Unfortunately, for some this translates into countless hours of thoughts that are entirely self-centered.

People who have spent years, even decades, struggling with obesity may find that they think about (rather, worry about) some aspect of that struggle on a daily basis. Is this God's plan for our thought life? I think not. We are told, "Whatever is true, whatever is noble, whatever is right, whatever is pure, whatever is lovely, whatever is admirable—if anything is excellent or praiseworthy—think about such things" (Phil. 4:8).

It is true that some people are totally obsessed with food. But along with food obsessions there is also the tendency to become obsessed with body weight, size, and appearance. When this is the case, the preoccupation is neither excellent nor praiseworthy, but it reflects a self-centeredness and vanity that are not befitting a disciple of Jesus Christ. Sure, we're entitled to become a little self-conscious about our weight when we receive the invitation for the high school reunion, but it's a far more serious matter when our body weight and appearance becomes the prevailing topic of our thought life. When this is the case, our motivation needs careful scrutiny.

For Christians, the motivation behind leading a healthy lifestyle must be pure. We should strive to honor our bodies, the temple of the Holy Spirit, through proper nutrition, exercise, and rest. We should strive for a level of spiritual maturity where everything we do—from the complicated to the mundane—reflects such biblical virtues as discipline, moderation, and temperance. And finally, we should glorify God by manifesting all the fruits of the Spirit, including self-control. When we live with these priorities, our motivation to maintain a healthy lifestyle is no longer self-centered but God-centered. Then weight loss comes first by way of a change of heart, followed by the tangible evidence of healthier lifestyle choices.

If, however, our desire to lose weight is fueled by a quest to achieve some standard of "acceptance" established by society, then we have missed the mark as believers, and we are doing exactly what Paul advised against—thinking of ourselves more highly than we ought.

In recent years, a number of support groups have been created for overweight and obese people. Their goals are to encourage their members to develop a positive attitude about their size and to tear down the discrimination and negative stereotypes that prevail against overweight and obese people. However, their approach is often counterproductive.

What often happens is that instead of placing *less* emphasis on body weight, many of these groups end up giving *more* attention to it. While their mission may be to someday reach a point where members are accepted for who they are, not what they weigh, achieving the mission becomes impossible if the very ones striving for it are obsessed with their outward appearance.

What is an effective way to guard against becoming overly concerned with body weight and physical appearance? Random acts of kindness. Serving others. Give, give, then give some more. This unlikely secret to achieving your weight loss goal is powerful because demonstrating kindness through acts of service is beneficial not only to the recipient but also to the giver. As you choose to give the fruit of the Spirit of kindness to others, your life will be enriched immeasurably.

Daily Prayer

> *Lord, I ask today that You examine my heart and purify my motives. Help me to guard my heart against self-centeredness and to place the needs of others above my own. Help me to become a vessel of kindness to a hurting world.*

HEALTH FACT OF THE DAY
DAY FIFTEEN

A 2007 study in the *New England Journal of Medicine* found that a person's chances of becoming obese increased by 57 percent if he or she had a friend who became obese.[1]

WHAT WOULD JESUS THINK?

Do nothing out of selfish ambition or vain conceit, but in humility consider others better than yourselves. Each of you should look not only to your own interest, but also to the interests of others.

—PHILIPPIANS 2:3–4

SEVERAL YEARS AGO, a discipleship campaign with the message "What Would Jesus Do?" swept through the church. The letters "WWJD" adorned bracelets, bumper stickers, T-shirts, bookmarks, and Bible covers. Believers and unbelievers alike posed this question to themselves and others, a question that was meant to sway us toward more Christlike behavior.

But actions can be deceiving, and one who truly wants to be a disciple must go a step beyond simply doing what Jesus would do. Actions begin with thoughts, and followers of Christ are to set a goal of even thinking the way Jesus would think. In his letter to the Philippians, the apostle Paul said, "Let this mind be in you, which was also in Christ Jesus" (Phil. 2:5, KJV). The New International Version translates it, "Your attitude should be the same as that of Christ Jesus." When our mind-sets and our attitudes emulate Christ, the right actions will follow.

So with that as a backdrop, let's examine some of our attitudes pertaining to food and pose the question, "WWJT" or "What would Jesus think?"

What would Jesus think about the amount of food produced in light of the number of people who go hungry?

Each day, our country produces 3,500 calories of food for every man, woman, and child. Granted, some of these calories are for things like cooking oil and condiments—things you wouldn't make into a meal.

But nevertheless, 3,500 calories is a huge amount of food, when you consider that active men with a normal BMI require approximately 2,500 calories, and active women with a normal BMI need about 2,000.

Children and the elderly need less, and, of course, the overweight and obese who are trying to lose weight should consume much less.

So, if we are producing this much food each day, why is it that so many don't have enough? Remember the five thousand Jesus fed with five loaves and two fish? And the four thousand He fed with seven loaves and a few little fish? He satisfied many with very little; we have abundance, yet many are left unsatisfied. What would Jesus think?

What would Jesus think about food advertising?

In 1971 a McDonald's ad that said, "You deserve a break today" ranked number five in the top one hundred advertisements of the twentieth century. Burger King's "Have it your way" from 1973 ranked number twenty-four. The overwhelming success of both ad campaigns is evident in the fact that we still remember them now, over thirty years later.

But the messages in these ads (and certainly the messages in more recent food promotions) are not entirely in keeping with a Christian perspective. Our daily verse even runs contrary: avoiding selfish ambition and looking out for the interest of others do not line up with having it your way and feeling entitled to a break today. How much have we allowed ourselves to be influenced by tempting advertisements for foods we ought to restrict or avoid? If we consider the regularity with which we purchase these foods, the answer would be that we've been *tremendously* influenced. So when it comes to how we decide what we'll eat, do we have the mind of Christ or the mind of the world? What would Jesus think?

What would Jesus think about families eating in separate rooms?

The Bible gives the account of how Jesus used mealtime as a time for conversation. He engaged in dialogue to teach, admonish, and correct. We're told of meals shared with special friends, as well as meals shared with Pharisees, Sadducees, and scribes—those whose intents were wicked.

In Deuteronomy we are instructed to pass down God's precepts to the next generation: "These commandments that I give you today are to be upon your hearts. Impress them on your children. Talk about them when you sit at home and when you walk along the road, when you lie down and when you get up" (Deut. 6:6–7). Certainly mealtime—a time we "sit at home"—is the ideal time for us to fulfill this commandment.

Current trends show that families are sharing fewer meals with one another, a trend that is more pronounced in low-income households. There are proven benefits to eating together, especially for teens. Teens who regularly share meals with their families are less likely to smoke, use alcohol and drugs, get into fights, or think about suicide. They are also more likely to delay sexual activity, and they do better academically than teens who eat separated from their families. Research also shows that children who eat with their parents have a higher intake of fruits and vegetables.[1]

But despite these benefits, only forty percent of American children aged twelve to seventeen eat with their families six to seven days a week. What would Jesus think?

What would Jesus think about twenty-four-hour drive-through availability?

Just how many people really need to eat at two o'clock in the morning? How many at 3:00 a.m.? More and more we see fast-food restaurants with drive-through lanes that are open all night long. Creating a need where none existed is a brilliant marketing strategy. But do we fall for this persuasion and eat at any time of day or night because the food is available, even to the detriment of our health? Is that the mind of Christ? Remember, it was Christ who said, "Therefore I tell you, do not worry about your life, what you will eat or drink; or about your body, what you will wear. Is not life more important than food, and the body more important than clothes?" (Matt. 6:25). Supersize at midnight? What would Jesus think?

Maintaining a healthy lifestyle is contingent upon not only our actions but also our thoughts. We must scrutinize the way we think about things; even subtleties we might take for granted in the way we eat and our activity level. We are told to "take captive every thought to make it obedient to Christ" (2 Cor. 10:5). *Every thought* includes those things we'd consider mundane or insignificant. When we learn to do this, then our actions will reflect our thinking, and we'll experience victory in our health.

Daily Prayer

Dear Lord, I humbly submit my entire life to You—my thoughts, words, and actions. I thank You that, through Christ, my thoughts can be renewed so that they help me to make lifestyle changes for better health, and that they will no longer work to hinder me.

HEALTH FACT OF THE DAY

DAY SIXTEEN

Ronald McDonald was the number two advertising icon of the twentieth century, second to the Marlboro Man. He has helped McDonald's become the dominant fast-food chain in the world, and his face is recognized by close to 96 percent of American children.[2]

DAY SEVENTEEN

AMBASSADORS FOR CHRIST

*Not so with you. Instead, whoever wants to become great among
you must be your servant, and whoever wants to be first must be
your slave—just as the Son of Man did not come to be served,
but to serve, and to give his life as a ransom for many."*

—MATTHEW 20:26–28

OUR VERSE FOR today gives Jesus's words after James and
John's mother asked Him to assign her sons honorable positions in the kingdom. This was not just the request of a
doting mother; it seems the two disciples wanted prominent positions
for themselves just as their mother did. Jesus's response was unconven-
tional. He told them greatness rests in serving, and eminence requires
us to rank others first.

As Christians, we have placed our faith in the atoning work of Jesus
and are indwelt by the Holy Spirit, who enables us to live in a manner
that exemplifies Christ. A true believer's heart, like the heart of Christ,
is devoted to others. Giving, serving, sacrifice, and placing the needs
of others above our own is the call for every believer. These things are
done without a hidden agenda, having no *desire* to receive, even though
we are promised rewards. This truth is contrary to what is heard from
many pulpits, where the message going forth in our time promotes
"self" to the point of error. Listening to some contemporary messages,
one would think Christ came to make us rich, prominent, comfortable…and fat.

For reasons beyond our physical health, we must break this detrimental way of thinking and embrace the true message of Christ. The
shackles of selfishness are evident in so many aspects of our lives. Self-
centeredness causes us to stray from the biblical marriage model, and
the divorce rate in the church equals that in the world. Self-centeredness
persuades us to forsake good stewardship of our finances and causes us
to overspend rather than tithe, give, and save. So debt, bankruptcy, and
foreclosures have devastated the church. And self-centeredness will

cause us to yield to the cravings of the flesh nature, which wants to overindulge in food and lead a sedentary existence. It should come as no surprise, then, that believers have the highest incidence of obesity and overweight.

This week is devoted to keeping the right attitude about our Christian lifestyle in general, and food and exercise in particular. One of our goals is to get rid of "self" when it comes to food—self-centeredness, self-indulgence, and selfishness. Jesus made it clear in His teachings that a "me first" attitude is not in keeping with the kingdom of God.

The apostle Paul, in 2 Corinthians, identifies Christians as "ambassadors for Christ" (2 Cor. 5:20, KJV). An ambassador is a delegate, an agent serving the one who commissioned him. As such, he is expected to fully represent the one in authority. Paul uses this description in the context of our responsibility to proclaim the gospel message of reconciliation to the entire world. But our words alone are insufficient because actions speak louder than words. Our message becomes inconsequential if we, as messengers, do not bear the appearance of Jesus Christ in our behavior. We need the world to see us as ambassadors, not hypocrites. An ambassador for Christ is not self-centered.

With this call in mind, let's look at how we "represent" Christ in terms of His self*less*ness when it comes to food, specifically when we eat out. With one out of five meals eaten outside the home and 925,000 restaurants at our disposal, I think it is indeed worthwhile to examine how we portray Christ in three specific areas to those we encounter in eating establishments. I hope that in doing so, we're better able to keep the right attitude when it comes to food.

- *Patience.* This is the fourth fruit of the Holy Spirit listed in Galatians 5:22. It is also a quality of love according to 1 Corinthians 13:4. But what happens to this attribute at a buffet? If the line moves slowly, Lord help the faithful servers. Indignant sighs, curt remarks, and a general air of displeasure prevail—even at church gatherings! A disappointing minority of people will make a habit of waiting for the line to dissipate while they engage in meaningful conversation with those present. Most choose to spend fellowship time standing in line, silently self-absorbed, waiting (impatiently) for another chance to eat.

- *Kindness.* I am certain the Holy Spirit is grieved—regularly—by how we react when waiters and waitresses make innocent mistakes, or if the food we are served is not to our liking. Kindness, like patience, is a fruit of the Spirit and a manifestation of love. As such, it should be part of our nature, no matter what the circumstances. But men and women who work in the food service industry will attest that when it comes to food, those professing Christ are prone to exchange kindness for anger and hostility if the food served does not meet their expectations.

- *Contentment.* We know God blesses us with food for our nourishment, our enjoyment, and as a means for enhancing fellowship. The primary reason for eating together is not the food per se, but for the opportunity to grow in unity with one another. Have you ever been to a Christian gathering where a spirit of discontentment *about the food* marred the fellowship? "This doesn't taste right"; "I'm still hungry"; "This was too cold"; "I didn't like how this was seasoned"; "They should have asked Miss So-and-So to make the cake. I like her cakes." I can only imagine what we would say if, sitting on the side of the mountain, we were passed bread and fish from the hands of the disciples: "I'll bet they didn't wash their hands—and shouldn't he be wearing a hairnet?"

In all things, let God be glorified. We are called to be ambassadors of Jesus Christ, to bear His image wherever we are and in everything we do. This is how God's kingdom is advanced.

Daily Prayer

Father, I have but one desire, and that is to glorify You. I ask that You help me to change my attitude so that I crucify self-centeredness and become an ambassador who represents You well.

HEALTH FACT OF THE DAY

DAY SEVENTEEN

The consumption of soft drinks increased by 61 percent in U.S. adults from 1977 to 1997,[1] and it more than doubled in children and teens from 1977–1978 to 1994–1998.[2] Higher consumption of sugar-sweetened drinks is associated with weight gain and an increase in the risk of developing type 2 diabetes.

DAY EIGHTEEN

THE MIRACLE OF SERVING OTHERS

*Consider it pure joy, my brothers, whenever you face trials of
many kinds, because you know that the testing of your faith develops
perseverance. Perseverance must finish its work so that you may be
mature and complete, not lacking anything.*

—JAMES 1:2–4

A S WE CONTINUE to devote this week to our attitude, I'd like
to share a real-life story to demonstrate the power that comes
through meeting the needs of others.

Several years ago, my sister developed severe pain throughout her
body, along with some other disturbing symptoms. She consulted a
number of physicians, who ordered a battery of blood tests and a variety
of X-rays. All of us were concerned that she might have a disease like
lupus or rheumatoid arthritis, but her physical examination and the
results of her laboratory tests did not provide us with a specific diagnosis. So ultimately, she was prescribed a number of pain medications
and anti-inflammatory drugs without knowing what was wrong with
her. To make matters worse, the medications had troubling side effects
and barely controlled her pain.

Naturally, she became frustrated with the medical doctors she'd
consulted, so she sought the advice of chiropractors, acupuncturists,
and even a massage therapist. But they too were perplexed. She looked
for information at the library and on the Internet without any success.
Her symptoms waxed and waned in intensity but never disappeared. She
was experiencing pain on a daily basis, and it didn't take long before she
went from simply being concerned and uncomfortable to being totally
consumed by her problem. She couldn't understand why she'd been given
such a "thorn in the flesh" with which to contend.

For some reason, at the height of her frustration, my sister decided
to enroll in a hospice training program offered at a nearby hospital.
This program trained volunteers to assist terminally ill patients and
their families. The volunteers were expected to help out with tangible

needs such as house cleaning and cooking. But the program was also designed to train them in ways to best serve their patients, walking with them through the dying process. Over time, they were expected to build solid relationships with the patients and family members, such that their presence and words of comfort might ease the pain and help them come to terms with their loss. In short, these volunteers received training in showing kindness.

When my sister began serving dying people in this capacity, a miraculous thing happened. No, her pain didn't go away, but something even more significant occurred. Through sharing with others and demonstrating the fruit of the Spirit of kindness, she was able to put her own problems into perspective. You may be familiar with the saying that poignantly observes, "I cried because I had no shoes, until I met a man who had no feet." When my sister washed the feet—both literally and figuratively—of people with problems far more serious than hers, her own physical problem became more bearable.

Consider this: if there is one thing that distinguishes us from our grandparents, it is that, in general, our grandparents had a higher tolerance for pain. Our standard of living and our quality of life have improved dramatically in only a few generations. We are now able to treat diseases that were once uniformly fatal. Likewise, it is now a rare tragedy for a woman to die in childbirth, though this was once a common outcome.

And it hasn't been too long ago that people spent many years of their life working in places that were physically unsafe or that exposed them to toxic chemicals. But while our grandparents endured great trials, they were not as inclined as we are today to seek an explanation for their pain. Simply put, suffering was just a part of life.

Today, however, our living standards are more comfortable, and as a result, our tolerance for pain is much lower. Along with that low threshold for pain, philosophies of today serve to justify in us an inordinate need to know why. "Why did God allow this to happen?" "Why, if He loves me, would He subject me to this?" "Why me, when I've tried to do right all my life?" Suffering is no longer accepted as a part of life; it is seen as an exceptional circumstance for which we deserve an explanation.

How did this happen? How is it that trials that would have been handled in stride by our grandparents shake us to the foundation of our souls? Why do we become so frustrated and angry when faced with a difficult life situation? I've concluded the answer is attributable in part to the prevalent New Age philosophy of today that encourages the exaltation of self.

One common thread in the New Age doctrine is the aggrandizement of mankind. Some of the teaching equates man's nature with the divine nature of God. It goes a step beyond the Christian doctrine, which says that the Spirit of God abides in a follower of Christ and instead asserts that man himself is divine. The essence of the teaching lies in its underlying premise of self-centeredness—my needs, my issues, my good, and my comfort. Consequently, when faced with a challenge, the person who follows New Age theology—consciously or unconsciously—feels entitled to an explanation.

Though self-centeredness may be at the core of New Age theology, self-centeredness is not Christian doctrine. Rather, a Christian lifestyle presumes that we *refrain* from selfish thinking and selfish behavior. The Bible never says that believers will be exempt from suffering, but it *does* encourage us to guard against becoming overwhelmed by our circumstances. As James indicates in our verse for today, Christians are to *expect* trials and, when they come, *endure* them and *grow* from the experience.

The fruit of the Spirit of kindness is that special fruit we demonstrate to others as "brotherly kindness." Focusing on serving others gives us a wonderful perspective and helps us to handle our trials in a manner that is Christlike. When kindness is richly manifested in us, it gives us the power to exchange our question of "Why me, Lord?" for a humble "Thank You, Lord." The problems of obesity and being overweight have the propensity to cause our focus to be self-centered. Showing kindness to others helps to protect us against this defeating self-absorption.

Daily Prayer

Father, I am grateful for the kindness You have shown me by providing a way for my salvation through Jesus Christ. Because of this kindness, I now have an eternal hope. Lord, I pray that You help me to maintain a right perspective in all things and that You plant in me a desire to meet the needs of others above my own.

HEALTH FACT OF THE DAY

DAY EIGHTEEN

A 2006 study suggests that weight gained during the adult years, specifically the years since menopause, can increase the risk for breast cancer in postmenopausal women, while weight loss after menopause is associated with a decreased risk.[1]

DON'T LET FOOD ADVERTISING
THROW YOU OFF

When goods increase, they are increased that eat them...
—ECCLESIASTES 5:11, KJV

THERE WAS NO obesity epidemic in ancient Palestine when Solomon was king. Nevertheless, Solomon, in profound wisdom, gives us this truth from the Book of Ecclesiastes that can be applied to the food industry of the twenty-first century, specifically in terms of America's obesity crisis.

While this proverb speaks to basic economic precepts like supply and demand, it also hints at such negative tendencies of the flesh as indulgence, discontentment, and gluttony. In our era the proverb is manifested, in part, through the power of advertising. With food being ever present and ever abundant, "they that eat them" are prone to do so after they've been bombarded with billboards, jingles, glossy ads, and commercial breaks.

Thirty billion dollars is spent each year on food advertising. Most of this amount goes toward television ads. And since television viewing starts in childhood (unfortunately, sometimes from infancy), our children have become prime targets for the food industry. Children are heavily persuaded to eat the very foods that should be limited or eliminated from their diets.

When it comes to advertising, there are currently no regulations in place that would mandate an equal representation of foods or require that the foods proven to be beneficial to our health are promoted just as heavily as those without any significant health benefits. Consider, for instance, the dollars budgeted for the National Cancer Institute's (NCI) "5 A Day" campaign versus the dollars spent to advertise soft drinks and candy.

The NCI had $1 million allocated for ads to remind us to eat at least five servings of fruits and vegetables each day. This is good, sound advice backed by scientific data. If we all adhered to it, the health of the nation would undoubtedly improve. But compare that to the figures from a decade ago, when $115.5 million was spent to advertise soft drinks and $10–50 million was spent promoting candy bars. I'd venture to say the average child is ten to fifty times more likely to ask for candy over fruit. Yes, advertising is highly effective.

I have subscribed to *Cooking Light* magazine for years. It helps to keep me from cooking the same meals over and over again and falling into a culinary rut. But every now and then, I'm a bit taken aback by some of the ads they run. Of course, I understand that any periodical relies heavily on advertising dollars to finance the magazine, but on more than a few occasions, I've been surprised that *Cooking Light*, a health-conscious magazine, would run food advertisements encouraging unhealthy eating, even suggesting that it's OK to forfeit self-control for the sake of taste.

Several years ago, I found two ads that I still use when I teach on the subject of temptation in advertising. One of the ads, sponsored by the American Dairy Association, shows an illuminated refrigerator case containing several blocks of cheese in a dimly lit room. The slogan reads, "Ahh, the power of cheese." The other one is from Nabisco promoting devil's food cookies from SnackWell's. The background of the ad is flaming red, and the caption reads, "Go ahead. Worship the Devil's Food."

Invariably, the initial response I get when I show these ads is fairly neutral. Some will even comment on the clever format and the play on words. But as we discuss them in more depth, specifically focusing on the power of words and the power of suggestion (two mainstays in successful advertising), everyone comes to appreciate the ads from a different perspective.

The first one from the American Dairy Association legitimizes indulgence by implying that some types of foods exert an influence beyond our control. There is some unexplainable, ethereal force that compels us to eat them. When we read the ad and see the rather spooky illuminated refrigerator, we feel justified in indulging ourselves with cheese. After all, the ad tells us it not only has power, but also it is powerful enough to make us go, "Ahh." The only thing left to do under the circumstances is to accept one's frailties and give in: "Now I understand why I lose control when it comes to cheese—it has supernatural power!"

The second ad not only encourages us to relinquish self-control when it comes to cookies, but (at least from a Christian's perspective) it also breeches on demonism, even to the point of condoning idolatry. I was not amused but offended by the ad. The very notion that we should worship *anything* other than God (and certainly something of the devil) goes against basic Judeo-Christian values—precepts as fundamental as the Ten Commandments.

Some might argue that I am overreacting, that it is only a harmless ad for chocolate cookies and not a call to join a cult or practice witch-craft. But my point is this: we cannot underestimate the effectiveness of advertising and its ability to persuade us to yield to temptation. Adver-tising works and it works well. For many, persistent weight gain is proof of advertising's effectiveness. And since we cannot avoid it, it's imperative that we remain on guard.

When approaching food advertisement, we should always be cognizant of how we are influenced. We must also appreciate the power of words. In the first chapter of Genesis, the phrase "And God said" is found over and over again. So with just a few words, God spoke the world into existence. I say this only to remind us of the power of words, a concept the advertising industry understands and uses to its advantage.

Most advertising relies on word power, and the food industry is no exception. Jingles and slogans for food are highly effective tools that can even keep us thinking about the product all day long. I remember back in January 1984, when Wendy's award-winning "Where's the beef?" campaign swept the nation. Everyone kept asking the question, "Where's the beef?" And apparently we didn't just inquire about its location—we found it! That year was one of the most successful sales years in Wendy's history.

According to the 1999 "Advertising Century" report (available at AdAge.com), half of the top ten slogans of the twentieth century were for foods or beverages:[1]

- Coca-Cola: "The pause that refreshes"
- Miller Lite: "Tastes great, less filling"
- Maxwell House: "Good to the last drop"
- Wheaties: "Breakfast of champions"
- Wendy's: "Where's the beef?"

Likewise, the top ten jingles of the century were well represented by food and beverages:

- McDonalds: "You deserve a break today."
- Pepsi-Cola: "Pepsi Cola hits the spot."

- Campbell's: "Mmm, mmm good"
- Oscar Meyer: "I wish I was an Oscar Meyer wiener."
- Coca-Cola: "It's the real thing."

And if we consider the top one hundred advertising slogans of the century, Coca-Cola landed three out of the top one hundred:

- "The pause that refreshes" (1929)—ranked #2
- "It's the real thing" (1969)—ranked #53
- "Always Coca-Cola" (1993)—ranked #86

Along with the slogans and jingles we hear, successful advertising also uses our sense of sight. The adage "A picture is worth a thousand words" is used effectively to promote sales. The food industry has used imagery in a powerful way. Of the top ten advertising icons of the twentieth century, the food industry holds claim to seven:

- Ronald McDonald
- The Green Giant
- Betty Crocker
- The Pillsbury Doughboy
- Aunt Jemima
- Tony the Tiger
- Elsie the Cow

Slogans and jingles combined with imagery and icons are the foundations for effective advertising. The combined approach of sight and sound succeeds in keeping food and beverages at the forefront of our thoughts. The ads then go on to persuade us to eat more and to eat often. But this does not reflect who we are called to be. Anything that encourages self-indulgence and anything that suggests we abandon discipline, moderation, and self-control should be resisted. And *this* is God's will for us—not having it our way, but having it His way.

Daily Prayer

Lord, I pray that You grant me wisdom and discernment when it comes to food advertising. Don't let me become so proud that I erroneously think it cannot influence my behavior. Help me to remain humble, and to always seek Your face so that I might resist temptation.

HEALTH FACT OF THE DAY

DAY NINETEEN

A study of nine- and ten-year-old children in Australia indicated that more than half of them believed that Ronald McDonald knows best what children should eat.[2]

YOUR ATTITUDE IS SHOWING

See that no one is sexually immoral, or is godless like Esau, who
for a single meal sold his inheritance rights as the oldest son.

—HEBREWS 12:16

I WISH IT WERE possible for you to close your eyes and still read
because I want to engage you in an exercise that requires you to use
your imagination. But since that's not possible, just try to envision
this scenario in your mind as you read along.

Imagine you and your family go out to dinner to your favorite restaurant after a wonderful Sunday service. This restaurant specializes in one
of your favorite foods, and of course, this is what you order. You enjoy
it immensely, just as you have during past visits. For me, I imagine that
special food might be key lime pie. But please select your favorite—whether
it's a main course or dessert—and think of it being perfectly prepared and
simply delicious.

Since you are aware that restaurant portions tend to be too large,
and you are diligent about limiting your serving sizes, you finish only
half and ask the waitress to bring you a carryout container. Your family
praises you for such impressive self-control to which you reply, "To God
be the glory!" You carefully place the remaining half of this delightful
food into the Styrofoam container, already thinking about when you
might finish it off.

The next morning you're off to the office, and you arrive to the typical
Monday morning chaos, only this particular morning you're confronted
with not just chaos, but an especially grueling day. When the day is finally
over, you get into your car for your journey home. You tune in to the
traffic report and learn that your usual forty-minute commute will take
an hour and a half because of various accidents and road construction.

You feel your neck muscles tighten and a faint throbbing in your
temples signals the start of a tension headache. You can't wait to get home
to relax and change into some comfy clothes. You've already planned out

the evening meal but, prior to preparing it, you've determined to unwind a bit and enjoy the contents of your Styrofoam container.

So you take off your suit and heels and put on a pair of sweats and slippers and head to the refrigerator. But when you open the door, your container is not there. You shift a few items around but—alas—no Styrofoam. You go to the garbage receptacle and there it lies. Empty. What happens next?

I've presented this scenario to audiences on several occasions, and the response is always revealing. Many people honestly admit they'd respond with some degree of anger (and dishonest folks say they'd feel great about the opportunity to be a blessing). The problem is that too many of us would not follow the biblical advice to be angry and yet do not sin (Eph. 4:26), but would allow food to generate in us an anger that would actually lead to sin.

One can envision the very peace of the home being destroyed through harsh words and foul attitudes. Some would hold a grudge the following day, or even days later, feeling perfectly justified. Of course, the incident would be kept on record for future confrontations—"Your problem is that you only think of yourself. Remember when you ate my food?"

I've had people justify a sinful response by pointing out that food was just the *symptom* of a deeper problem resting in the offender. They rationalize that the source of their anger wasn't that they missed out on eating restaurant leftovers, but stemmed from the audacious self-centeredness of the narcissist who ate their food. Keep in mind, the flesh nature has mastered the art of rationalization. The bottom line is that in this scenario, many would commit the sin of lust for food.

This carnality is what the writer of the Book of Hebrews warns against in today's verse. This account of Esau is found in Genesis 25:27–34. Here we find Esau coming home from the field extremely hungry, and he sees that his twin brother Jacob has prepared some stew. Now, Jacob could easily be described as an audacious, self-centered narcissist. Yes, Jacob was a deceiver who set up his brother for a fall. Jacob is not off the hook in wrongdoing, just as the one who ate the food in our scenario would not be off the hook. But the first step in repentance is to resist the urge to blame. We must first examine ourselves for the tendencies of Esau before pointing out the tendencies of Jacob that we see in others.

Esau's desire to satisfy his flesh caused him to forfeit what should have been precious to him—his birthright. And while our culture is different in terms of the birthright and the blessing due the firstborn, the underlying issue has not changed. Introspection requires us to ask ourselves, "What precious thing are we willing to forfeit in order to satisfy our cravings?"

Our scenario might reveal in some a willingness to forfeit a peaceful home and peaceful relationships with the ones we love. Some will see a willingness to become bitter and unforgiving over food. It might point out the tendency to harbor an unloving disposition since love is not rude, is not easily angered, and keeps no record of wrongs according to 1 Corinthians 13.

But don't limit yourself to this imaginary scenario. Include in your reflections a careful examination of your "real-life" responses. Are you willing to forfeit the call to selflessness by rushing to the head of the buffet line? Do you become impatient with the folks who beat you there if they take too long to serve themselves? Are your words harsh to waiters and waitresses if the food you ordered was not to your liking? Do you forfeit a kind and generous spirit by never sharing?

Our attitude toward food is vitally important in determining whether we will have long-term success with weight loss. But, more importantly, our attitude toward food also reveals our heart. Ask yourself: "When it comes to food, am I more like Christ or more like Esau?"

Daily Prayer

Lord, I ask that You help me maintain the right attitude about food. Let it always be for me the blessing You intended it to be. May I never allow it to cause me to sin.

HEALTH FACT OF THE DAY

DAY TWENTY

Engaging in regular exercise will cut the risk for developing type 2 diabetes by 16 to 50 percent. Studies also suggest that regular exercise may delay the onset of Alzheimer's disease.[1]

DAY *TWENTY-ONE*

THE JOY OF THE LORD

Why are you downcast, O my soul? Why so disturbed within me? Put your hope in God, for I will yet praise him, my Savior and my God.

—PSALM 42:11

EVERY NOW AND then, we all feel a little down and out. Life is often filled with trouble, and discouraging circumstances abound, so occasional feelings of sadness are quite normal. We may, like the psalmist, find ourselves asking, "Why are you downcast, O my soul? Why so disturbed within me?" It is normal to have times when we feel "downcast" in the face of life's challenges.

Unfortunately, some people feel more than just an occasional bout with "the blues." For them, the feelings of depression are overwhelming and unexplained. They are consumed with a sense of sadness that has no identifiable source. In these instances, the symptoms cannot be attributed to those normal, transient periods of feeling down and out. Instead, they indicate a clinical depression.

The person suffering with depression may feel sad, helpless, and irritable. Changes in sleeping patterns are also common, taking the form of insomnia, excessive sleep, or restless sleep. In some cases, depression may distort the thought processes, even to the point of causing delusions and hallucinations. The appetite may be affected, resulting in either anorexia or overeating. Fatigue and a lack of interest in the activities once enjoyed are also symptoms of clinical depression. Job performance and school performance suffer because of an inability to concentrate. In severe cases, there are recurring thoughts of suicide and death.

Signs of depression can be elusive. It often goes undiagnosed because many people don't attribute their symptoms to depression. They think they have some other condition, like the flu or anemia. This explains why a great number of depressed people first seek help from a primary care physician—an internist or a family doctor—and not a psychiatrist. They believe their symptoms are the result of an organic, rather than a psychiatric, disorder.

Obesity and depression can sometimes go hand in hand. It is estimated that about 25 to 30 percent of obese patients who seek weight-reduction treatment suffer with a significant depression or other psychological disturbance.[1] Many of these patients have a binge-eating disorder, a fairly common eating disorder occurring in 2 percent of the general population, more commonly in women.

Since both obesity and depression are common conditions, it's often difficult to determine if one is related to the other or if the person afflicted with both conditions simply has two common problems occurring simultaneously but totally unrelated to one another. It's tempting to try to figure out the "chicken and egg" dynamic—did the depression make the person obese, or did the obesity make the person depressed? But while it may be interesting to know the "source" condition, the answer is purely academic since the solution is the same—treat the depression.

It is nearly impossible to succeed in losing weight in the face of untreated depression because it influences both eating behavior and the attitude toward exercise. Depression leads to overeating when food is used to soothe its symptoms. And depression destroys motivation, which is so necessary to prompt regular exercise.

Drugs have been developed as one form of treatment for depression. One category of antidepressant drugs is known as the selective serotonin reuptake inhibitors (SSRI). They alter the brain's concentration of the neurotransmitter serotonin. Some of the drugs in this particular class were found to have an interesting side effect—they suppress the appetite. This gives credence to the observation that mood and eating behavior are linked. Medications work well, but they are not the only forms of therapy available. Behavioral therapy and psychotherapy—for groups or individuals—are also quite effective.

The medication issue is complicated by the well-known placebo effect. In a review of seventy-five clinical trials involving patients with major depressive disorders, the response to a placebo ranged from 10 to 50 percent. In about half of the trials, 30 percent or more of the patients who were taking a placebo showed a significant improvement in their depressive symptoms.[2] So even if the problem originates from a chemical imbalance, the solution to correcting the imbalance does not always require the use of prescription drugs.

I believe, for the Christian, even if medications and psychotherapy are used, the approach is incomplete without pursuing a greater understanding of the joy of the Lord. Joy extends beyond mere feelings of gladness. Joy, as a fruit of the Spirit, resides in the Christian; it is present at all times, regardless of negative circumstances. So, how can it be that depression can overtake the person indwelt by joy?

We will not experience joy when we allow our circumstances and our emotions to prevail. Bad times and difficult days are inevitable, promised by Jesus Christ Himself. (See John 16:33.) But the circumstances of life, while challenging, are only temporary. The Christian has an eternal hope that outweighs the adversities of life, and this brings us joy. Likewise, if we refuse to forgive or if we harbor negative emotions like bitterness, envy, anger, and resentment, we have created within us the spiritual milieu for depression to reign.

I would encourage you if you have any signs or symptoms of depression to share your feelings with your health care provider or a mental health counselor. Seeking help does not mean you lack faith—it reveals a great measure of wisdom.

Daily Prayer

> *Lord, I ask that You open my eyes to the evidence of depression if it exists in me today. Please remove any pride that may hinder me from seeking help. I ask that You reveal to me how I have been swayed by my circumstances rather than trusting in You as my foundation. I pray that You reveal to me any sinful emotions that I have nurtured so that I can repent and be delivered.*

HEALTH FACT OF THE DAY
DAY TWENTY-ONE

Major depression is a risk factor for the development of coronary heart disease events in healthy people, and for adverse cardiovascular events in people with established heart disease. Depression is present in one of five patients with coronary heart disease and in one of three patients with congestive heart failure, yet the majority of cases are not recognized or appropriately treated.[3]

WEEKLY ASSESSMENT

My weight:	My BMI:	My waist size in inches:

I upheld my covenant by:

(Use a pencil and shade in the boxes starting from left to right to show how well you upheld your covenant this week.)

Less than 25%	25–49%	50–74%	75–99%	100%

VICTORIES: _____

_____

_____

_____

_____

_____

_____

PITFALLS: _____

_____

_____

_____

_____

_____

_____

Live in Grace

THE LETTER OF THE LAW

Do not think that I have come to abolish the Law or the Prophets;
I have not come to abolish them but to fulfill them.

—MATTHEW 5:17

ONCE A DEAR friend told me she had changed her morning routine: "Every day, before I eat breakfast, I drink a mixture of honey, lemon juice, and vinegar." I blended the flavors together in my mind and immediately asked her why in the world she would drink such a concoction, having a personal preference for hazelnut coffee to start my day. She told me she was drinking it in order to lose weight. Now, at the time she shared this with me, she hadn't lost any weight, despite her faithful adherence. And a few weeks later, when she apparently had had enough of this beverage, she still hadn't lost any weight.

I hear a fair share of weight loss testimonies—both successful and unsuccessful. What never ceases to amaze me is the tendency ingrained in us humans to look for a set of rules to follow. We, by nature, like a firm set of regulations; we want to know the parameters and stick to the guidelines, whatever they happen to be. I believe there is a measure of security found in following rules, and there is nothing wrong with wanting to feel secure. There is a problem, however, when our passion for guidelines causes us to miss the point. Unfortunately, we often fail to see the forest for the trees, so to speak.

When the original version of *Spiritual Secrets to Weight Loss* was released, a comment I received from readers (a comment I heard more often than I'd like) was that they read the book, they enjoyed the book, but they still didn't know what to eat. Now, there was some validity to this point, which is why the introduction of this revision includes some very basic information on food and exercise. But let's be honest. In this day and age, information on nutrition is widely and readily available from many different sources. We are saturated with good advice on healthy living from magazines, television, and the Internet. Insurance companies mail brochures, public schools send home flyers, libraries post bulletins, churches sponsor health fairs, and even the local supermarket pipes in the recommendation for "5 A Day" while you shop for groceries. The issue is not so much *ignorance* as it is a desire for *rules*. In other words, if you tell me exactly what to eat, when to eat, and how much to eat, I'll stick to it, and I'll expect to see results.

Our verse for today is taken from the Sermon on the Mount, found in the Gospel of Matthew. Jesus makes a point that would utterly confound the Pharisees, Sadducees, and scribes during His entire earthly ministry, and that was the distinction between a mere *adherence* to the law and an understanding of the *essence* of the law. Let me make it clear before we go any further that I am not in any way equating the friction that existed between Jesus and the religious leaders with our goal of making lifestyle changes for better health. My point is this: the religious leaders were so determined to stick to the *letter* of the law that they failed to comprehend the *spirit* of the law—the big picture. And this tendency to miss the big picture is exactly what we want to avoid when we make a decision to lose weight.

The big picture is not that you chew your food at a slower rate and take longer to complete a meal. Yes, that may be important in terms of satiety signals, but it is not the big picture. The big picture is not whether or not you eat past six o'clock in the evening. Yes, that may be a good practice, especially if you have acid reflux, but it is not the big picture. Making sure you drink a specified number of eight-ounce glasses of water each day is not the big picture, although we surely don't want to become dehydrated. Yet, these are the sorts of rules we are quick to follow, expecting results. Unfortunately, the truth of the matter is that unless we grasp the big picture, the rules don't do much in the long run. Just ask my friend who drank the honey, lemon juice, and vinegar each morning.

The big picture relates to the character traits (or character flaws) that prevent us from making permanent changes for better health. So if our daily menu (that is, what, when, and how much we'll eat and how it will be prepared) represents the *letter* of the law, then such attributes as self-control, discipline, moderation, sobriety, subjecting the flesh, and resisting temptation would represent the *essence* of the law.

With that analogy, it should be clear why diet plans are destined to fail unless attention is given to *why* the diet plan is needed in the first place. This would constitute the essence of the matter. Any dietician can prescribe a 1,200-, 1,400-, or 1,600-calorie meal plan, but no dietician can make us practice self-control. A popular diet might favor proteins over carbohydrates or vice versa, but no diet plan—no matter how popular—can tell us how to subject our flesh and resist temptation. We can tally points, and we can make exchanges, but neither points nor exchanges can teach us discipline and moderation.

One person may enjoy a slice of pie operating with a mature level of self-control, while another person may eat celery sticks and be severely lacking in self-control. The first person will enjoy the foods he or she eats yet maintain a healthy body weight; the second person will tolerate celery sticks for a season, then resume the bad habits that contributed to their weight problem, and in the long run find themselves weighing more than when they started.

Legalism hurt the ancient Palestinians, and it hurts us today. Never forget that it is the essence of the law that matters, and learning the essence comes by way of the Holy Spirit.

Daily Prayer
Father, I thank You for sending Your Son Jesus Christ to fulfill the law. Please help me to focus on those attributes such as self-control, moderation, and sobriety that are in keeping with my call as a disciple of Christ. I know when I grow in these areas I will be equipped to take control of my lifestyle for better health.

HEALTH FACT OF THE DAY
DAY TWENTY-TWO

A 2006 study of more than seven hundred adults at high risk for cardiovascular disease compared a low-fat diet to a Mediterranean diet supplemented with olive oil or nuts. After three months, the Mediterranean diet groups had lower blood glucose (sugar) levels, lower blood pressure, and an improved cholesterol profile compared with the low-fat group.[1]

DAY TWENTY-THREE

THE GRACE TO FORGIVE

"Forgive us our debts, as we also have forgiven our debtors. And lead us not into temptation, but deliver us from the evil one." For if you forgive men when they sin against you, your heavenly Father will also forgive you. But if you do not forgive men their sins, your Father will not forgive your sins.

—MATTHEW 6:12–15

AT THIS WRITING, the most recent data on the U.S. prevalence of obesity and overweight is from information collected in 2003–2004. Compared with the numbers from 1999–2000, there has been an increase in the prevalence in children and adolescents (both boys and girls, currently 17.1 percent overweight), as well as in men (now 31.1 percent obese). During this interval, no significant change was noted in women—as a group, we didn't gain significantly, neither did we lose.

Currently, the majority of the adult population is either overweight or obese. In adults (both women and men), 66.3 percent of the population is overweight as defined by a BMI of 25 or more; 32.2 percent is obese as defined by a BMI of 30 or more; and 4.8 percent falls into the category of extreme obesity with a BMI over 40.[1]

When we examine the population in specific groups rather than as a whole, there are significant differences noted in terms of age and especially in race. The following table shows the prevalence for women aged forty to fifty-nine. Notice the striking difference in the amount of obesity and overweight when broken down by race:

Women, aged 40–59:	Overweight: BMI 25 or more	Obesity: BMI 30 or more	Extreme Obesity: BMI 40 or more
Caucasian	65.3%	37.8%	7.0%
Hispanic	79.7%	48.3%	7.8%
African American	88.0%	57.5%	16.5%

I present these numbers to emphasize the point that the majority of the population is overweight and has been for many years. My point, however, in presenting them is not just for shock value. Our focus today is on forgiveness. What is the connection between health statistics and our need to forgive?

The fact is that there is a great deal of discrimination against people based on body weight in spite of the data that indicate most of the U.S. population is overweight and roughly one-third is obese. Stigmatization, stereotypes, and prejudices against the overweight and obese abound.

Obese people are more likely to be denied admission into college, they have more trouble renting a residence, and they are less likely to marry than normal-weight individuals.[2] Obesity may limit the opportunity for career advancement; it is also associated with decreased job earnings.[3] The negative stereotypes connected to excess body weight include laziness, stupidity, dishonesty, and poor hygiene.

There is a strong inverse relationship between obesity and socioeconomic status, especially in women. It is not entirely clear if obesity influences the socioeconomic status or if socioeconomic status influences body weight. It is also possible an outside factor influences both. Whatever the case, the association is clear and consistent. In a 1993 study, investigators tracked overweight adolescents for seven years into adulthood. Women who had been overweight teens had completed fewer years of school, were 20 percent less likely to be married, and had a lower household income and higher rates of poverty than the women who had not been overweight. This outcome was independent of their socioeconomic status as teens and also independent of their high school aptitude test scores. Other teens followed who were not overweight but had conditions like asthma, bone abnormalities, and a variety of chronic health conditions, and they did not experience these discrepancies upon becoming adults.[4]

Even the medical profession is guilty of harboring misconceptions based on weight. Medical students were found to have an almost uniformly negative reaction to extremely obese people, categorizing them as unpleasant, worthless, and bad. The students' attitudes did not change even after they spent some time working with obese patients.[5] Obese people are less likely to receive the standard of care for the early detection of cancer. Obese men and women are less likely to be screened for colon cancer, and obese women receive fewer mammograms and Pap smears

than women with a normal BMI, despite having a higher rate of breast
and cervical cancers.

This kind of stigmatization and mistreatment is certainly not in keeping
with how God wants people to be treated. Many times we as believers are
victimized by these prejudices, and deeply rooted feelings of hostility and
bitterness—feelings that might seem justified—are produced. However,
these responses are not pleasing to God. He expects us to process our
anger, to eliminate bitterness, and to forgive.

The Lord said that vengeance belongs to Him (Deut. 32:35). When we
feel the need to "get even," we are assuming the responsibility for what
God declared was His right exclusively. Our verse for today is taken from
the Sermon on the Mount, where Jesus gives us the Lord's Prayer. In it, He
takes time to emphasize how important forgiveness is to God. Just as God
has forgiven us, so we are required to forgive those who hurt us.

We, as recipients of God's grace, are required to bless others with the
same loving-kindness. Turn your hurts over to the Lord. Don't harbor
negative feelings against those who offend you. It will do nothing other
than hinder your progress toward lifestyle modification. An unforgiving
person plants seeds of bitterness into his or her own soul. When bitterness takes root, our mental and physical health suffers. So, if our goal
is to improve our health, then harboring a spirit of unforgiveness is the
equivalent to shooting oneself in the foot. It is counterproductive and,
more importantly, it is a sin.

The process of forgiveness may seem impossible to you, and your hurts
may seem too deep to resurface and deal with, but this is not something
you have to do alone. If you have been overweight or obese for a long
time, you may have wells of hurt, bitterness, and resentment to uncover
and deal with. It is wise to seek out help from a close, spiritually mature
friend who loves you, your accountability partner, a pastor, or even a
Christian counselor.

Forgiveness is an important step in this fifty-day renewal process that
cannot be overlooked. This is where you will find the grace you need to
forgive yourself as well and put the past behind you.

Know that the Lord is omniscient and omnipresent. He loves you, and
He knows precisely how others have treated you. But the Lord also sees
how you react to those who have wronged you, and above all, His expectation is that you forgive.

Daily Prayer

> *Dear Lord, You know every pain I experience, and You know the sting of prejudice and stigmatization. I thank You for giving me the grace to forgive those whose attitudes and behaviors toward me are based on negative stereotypes. I pray that You open their eyes to the truth and show them the error of their ways. Help me to forgive others as You have forgiven me.*

HEALTH FACT OF THE DAY
DAY TWENTY-THREE

Regular physical activity relieves symptoms of anxiety and depression and improves mood. In a study, researchers compared the effects of thirty minutes of walking compared to thirty minutes of quiet rest in forty adults with depression. Both groups showed lower scores for tension, anger, and fatigue, but only the exercise group had improved scores on measurements for "vigor" and "well-being."[6]

DAY TWENTY-FOUR

THE PEACE OF GOD

You will keep in perfect peace him whose mind is steadfast,
because he trusts in you.

—ISAIAH 26:3

STRESS, EITHER PHYSICAL or psychological, can influence eating behavior. We typically feel stress when we are subjected to circumstances that we feel powerless to change or control. When situations are under our control, they will not generate as much stress as when they are beyond our control.

While a certain degree of stress is an unavoidable part of living, extreme stress has a detrimental effect on our physical and mental health. Excessive stress depletes our bodies of nutrients, alters our hormonal and chemical balance, and disturbs our sleep cycle. The consequences of stress are not universal but vary from person to person. Those who are able to cope with stress are better off than those who don't cope well. The hallmark of an effective coping strategy is being able to stay relaxed no matter what the conditions.

There's an old saying: *Anyone who can remain calm in this situation does not fully understand the situation.* Some people are able to remain calm, no matter how serious the circumstances. They simply don't allow the challenges of life to overwhelm them. Other people appear to be calm, but instead of a true inner peace, they have artificially generated calmness through substances they use to help them cope. Some of these substances are illegal, like marijuana and heroin. The vast majority, however, are legal: prescription drugs, alcohol, tobacco and—in the case of the stress eater—food.

Those who rely on substances to generate peace come to the point where they depend on them, a dependence that is either physical (as in the case with alcohol and narcotics, where withdrawal from the substance causes potentially serious changes in the body) or psychological, as in the case with food. Whether physical or psychological, the end result is addiction and obsession.

120

While the person addicted to alcohol, tobacco, or drugs is sometimes chastised for their vice, the food addict usually goes unnoticed. Food doesn't alter our mood or influence our thoughts so that we cannot function normally, as do alcohol and some drugs. Eating is a socially acceptable activity, but the tendency to turn to food in response to stress can be just as addictive as the tendency to pour a drink or light up a cigarette.

What makes a person a stress eater? From a physiologic standpoint, stress should actually decrease, rather than increase, the appetite. Stress stimulates our bodies to release hormones triggering what is known as the "fight or flight" response. Our pulse quickens, our breathing rate increases, and blood is shifted from our digestive system and other internal organs to the muscles in our arms and legs.

The changes these hormones bring about prepare us to fight against, or run away from, whatever is causing the stress. In either event—whether the choice is to fight or to run—it's clearly no time to eat. And this is why many people will *lose* their appetites in times of stress.

However, this is not true of stress eaters. No matter what the physiology, when the heat is on, they eat. Most stress eaters share a common trait that may explain their reaction to stress: they are prone to closely monitor the way they eat. In general, the world is made up of two types of people: those who regulate their eating and those who don't. The latter eat whatever they want, whenever they want, and however much they want without a great deal of thought and are able to maintain a normal BMI in the process. If you're reading this book, chances are that you are not in that category. You are probably among the people who must set up restraints when it comes to food. This group is called *inhibited* eaters. It is this group, the people who must be mindful of their eating and must inhibit their impulses, who are prone to eat in response to stress.

What happens when inhibited eaters are confronted with stress? It weakens their resolve. Stress will deplete them of the energy they need to monitor their eating. And once the restraints are removed, they overeat.

Not all forms of stress will unleash the inhibited eater. Most commonly it is the type of stress that violates his or her sense of self-worth. The stress generated by an escalating crime rate, the high cost of living, or a broken-down car does not predispose the inhibited eater to overeat. These types of stressors don't challenge a person's sense of personal value.

On the other hand, the stress generated by the disparaging comments of a critical boss, the infidelity of a spouse, or the disrespectful behavior of children *will* trigger overeating. Stress that comes from detraction and condemnation strikes the identity and diminishes the self-esteem. It acts as a painful trigger for out-of-control eating.

Stress eaters will often deny their problem or underestimate the amount of food they actually eat. This denial may not be intentional—eating in response to stress is like a reflex; it's done without thinking.

When I encounter patients who deny that they eat under stress but I suspect that they do, I will have them maintain a food journal for a few weeks. This requires them to keep a log of everything they eat, no matter how insignificant. They record the date, time, and, most importantly, the circumstances associated with the eating.

If the journal is maintained honestly and consistently, it is always revealing. When we review it, we see right away those situations that prompted eating. We usually find a strong connection between stress and impulse eating. It also provides a good estimate of the number of calories consumed each day—a piece of information that is valuable for those patients who maintain they don't eat much.

Stress eaters use food to help them cope with the ups and downs of life. Food is a blessing; it cannot give us peace. True peace comes through a close relationship with God, and His Spirit gives us peace from within. The fruit of the Spirit of peace is an internal, not external, source of peace. As we become filled with God's peace, we won't need to resort to food or any substance to help reduce our stress levels. The Bible says God's peace surpasses our comprehension and protects our hearts and our minds (Phil. 4:7). It quiets the storms of life and helps us to stay unruffled through any situation.

Daily Prayer

Lord, I acknowledge You as Jehovah-Shalom, the God of peace. I am thankful for the peace You have given me through the fruit of the Spirit. I commit to keep my mind focused on You during the stressful situations I will encounter today, and I will not use food as a way to calm my spirit. I thank You for the promise to keep me in perfect peace if I keep my mind on You.

HEALTH FACT OF THE DAY
DAY TWENTY-FOUR

In healthy populations, studies show a connection between heart disease and type A personality, depression, anxiety, and high-stress employment.

LIBERTY AND OUR COMMITMENT TO OTHERS

"Everything is permissible"—but not everything is beneficial.
"Everything is permissible"—but not everything is constructive.
Nobody should seek his own good, but the good of others.

—1 CORINTHIANS 10:23–24

I N THE BOOK of 1 Corinthians, the apostle Paul answers questions and clarifies points of confusion for this young church located in a decadent, pagan city. The influence of the world had crept into the church, a problem we certainly face today.

One of the issues challenging these believers pertained to whether or not they should eat meat that had been sacrificed to idols. Paul begins his discussion on the matter in chapter 8: "So then, about eating food sacrificed to idols: We know that an idol is nothing at all..." (1 Cor. 8:4).

After making the point that idols are nothing, he goes on in verse 7 to remind the congregation that "not everyone knows this." But then Paul draws an interesting conclusion. He doesn't rebuke the ones within the congregation who are immature in their faith, the ones who don't know that good meat is good meat, whether it was offered on a pagan altar or not. He doesn't suggest they eat the meat in order to be economical, since frugality is a virtue and wastefulness reveals poor stewardship of God's resources. He doesn't advise the more mature Christians to just ignore those brothers with a weak conscience and enjoy their meal amongst themselves. But he gives this congregation a word of advice, and his point is profound. He says, "Be careful, however, that the exercise of your freedom does not become a stumbling block to the weak" (1 Cor. 8:9).

The apostle Paul does not focus on what categorizes the weak as weak; instead, he issues a challenge to the strong. He knows the burden to exemplify Christlike behavior is greater on those who are strong in the faith than it is on those who are weak. The liberty *in* Christ made eating meat from pagan altars completely acceptable. The love *of* Christ made eating meat from pagan altars completely *un*acceptable if doing so offended a brother who was not as spiritually mature.

As believers, we have liberty, but we also have a commitment to our brothers and sisters in Christ. If the exercise of my liberty becomes self-centered, such that I am seeking to fulfill my own needs over the needs of others, then I have misunderstood the essence of liberty.

How are we doing in terms of living out this concept in the body of Christ today? Specifically, has the exercise of our liberty been a stepping stone or a stumbling block to other believers? When it comes to the way we eat, I submit we have not been "careful," as the apostle Paul would say, in our regard for others.

When we know a brother or sister is trying to change bad eating habits to lose weight, or when we are with a brother or sister whom we know has a medical condition requiring dietary restriction, all too often our attitude is not one of "I care," but a selfish "Who cares?"

Because I am a physician with an interest in disease prevention through lifestyle modification, and because I am a church leader in my role as a pastor's wife, I draw more attention than I'd care to at events where a meal is served. Because of these two "hats," I am frequently invited to events where food is served.

Invariably, people will react to my presence in terms of what they choose to eat. The most common reaction I experience is shame and embarrassment from men and women over what types of foods or how much food they've placed on their plates. It seems I become their conscience incarnate, a convicting presence that can destroy appetites through generating guilt. I hate when this happens. The last thing I want to do is make anyone uncomfortable at a time meant for enjoyment and fellowship. So I make a habit of not looking at peoples' plates. Over the years, I have developed the skill of maintaining eye-to-eye contact and directing my attention toward anything other than the plate of the person to whom I'm speaking. Contrary to popular belief, I really don't like making people squirm.

There is a second reaction I receive that directly speaks to this issue of liberty: people evaluate *my* plate and comment on the types of foods and quantities *I* have selected. "Look, she's hardly eating anything," or "You're not going to try the macaroni and cheese?" or "That's all you want?" are typical comments.

My BMI and waist circumference are in the normal range, and my blood pressure, cholesterol, and blood glucose levels are all normal. I practice self-control and moderation so that if I overeat at one meal, I compensate for it by eating less for the remainder of the day. Likewise, if I eat foods I know are too high in saturated fat or sodium, or low in fiber, again, I balance this in how I eat later on.

I say this to make the point that at social events I have liberty to eat whatever I want—even macaroni and cheese—but I will *forfeit* my liberty for the sake of others. If even one person at such an event were hindered because they saw me eating what they need to restrict or avoid, then what is *permissible* to me would be neither beneficial nor constructive. I never want the exercise of my freedom to become a stumbling block for others.

Ask yourself: Is my behavior a help or a hindrance to others? I believe if we all took to heart and practiced what the Bible teaches, we'd see dramatic improvements in the health of the church.

Daily Prayer

> *Father, I thank You for the sacrificial death and resurrection of Jesus Christ, who sealed my liberty by releasing me from the bondage of sin. Please grant me wisdom in the exercise of my freedom. Help me to be obedient to Your Word and seek the good of others over my own.*

HEALTH FACT OF THE DAY

DAY TWENTY-FIVE

The typical Western diet, one high in refined grains, meat, fried foods, and diet soda, will increase the risk for developing the metabolic syndrome.[1]

BE CONTENT

*But godliness with contentment is great gain. For we brought
nothing into the world, and we can take nothing out of it. But if
we have food and clothing, we will be content with that.*

—1 TIMOTHY 6:6–8

GOD HAS FAITHFULLY shown Himself to be the One who provides for us and meets our every need, especially our need for food. Unfortunately, the natural tendency of man is not toward the gracious state of contentment but rather toward discontentment. This tendency is seen not just with food but also in every aspect of life. In today's verse, the apostle Paul mentions the importance of contentment in his instruction to Timothy, making it clear that it is how we ought to respond to having our basic needs met.

We know God has ordained that the earth provide us with plants and animals for food and clothing. Notice, however, that Paul's words neither qualify nor quantify these provisions. More often than not, however, we live in a state of profound error because we allow our contentment to be based upon the quality and the quantity of our provisions. In other words, we forfeit the blessed state of contentment through the pursuit of "more and better," when sometimes, our provisions fall into the "just enough" or even the "bare minimum" categories. Understand this: being dissatisfied with what we have does not mean God has compromised on His promises. This is demonstrated in the account of the children of Israel's wilderness experience.

After being miraculously released from slavery in Egypt, the Israelites found themselves in the wilderness. God, the One who delivered them from bondage, provided them with food to eat in the form of manna, a substance from heaven that bore the appearance of "thin flakes like frost on the ground" (Exod. 16:14). They collected it and ate it like bread. God was faithful in that they always had enough. He established this daily miracle after hearing them complain about not having anything to eat.

But the spirit of discontentment that prompted them to complain in the first place was not softened by the manna. They launched even more complaints about the bread from heaven, even revealing that the root of their dissatisfaction was they longed for the foods they ate while enslaved:

> …Again the Israelites started wailing and said, "If only we had meat to eat! We remember the fish we ate in Egypt at no cost—also the cucumbers, melons, leeks, onions and garlic. But now we have lost our appetite; we never see anything but this manna!"
>
> —Numbers 11:4–6

Certainly the Israelites had a reason to be grateful. First they were delivered from bondage, and now they were given the provisions of food and clothing. Remember, our daily verse tells us what ought to be enough to keep us satisfied, but a state of discontentment will invariably cloud our perception and even make us ungrateful for the blessings we experience each day. In the case of the Israelites, their food was provided as a daily miracle from heaven. The supernatural miracle that their food was exempt from natural laws requiring seeds, soil, water, and sunlight, but instead appeared from the sky through no effort on their part, should have been enough to silence complaints. The goodness of God moved Him to break the law of sowing and reaping on their behalf. But instead of responding with awe and thanksgiving, they grumbled.

The root of their discontentment was that they fou. restriction intolerable. This was a major problem in the Sinai wilderness, and it is a major problem today. God decided that the Israelites would live under a set of dietary restrictions. Their food was, at least for that season, manna. They were upset because limits were placed on what they could eat, and this was heightened by their awareness of what they were missing. Their testimony revealed how they enjoyed the pleasant taste of many different kinds of foods. Yet now, for reasons beyond their control, they were required to live under a set of guidelines whereby manna was the food of the day, every day. But since their flesh nature rejected it, they couldn't show gratitude for this miraculous provision.

The more things change, the more they stay the same—especially when it comes to the flesh nature. Weight loss requires us to restrict the amount of food we eat and set limits on the types of foods we eat. Moreover, for many medical conditions, the best management includes a set of dietary restrictions. Even those blessed with a normal body weight and no diet-related medical problems are wise in setting limits on what they eat in order to preserve their good health. The account from the first chapter of Daniel confirms there is nothing wrong with dietary restrictions. To the contrary, it is a good thing to set some parameters when it comes to what we eat.

Like the Israelites, we tend to let *restriction* cloud our eyes to *provision*. Manna was a wonderful provision deserving of praise and thanksgiving. Instead of praising God, the Israelites grumbled and complained because their carnal eyes were focused on what they were missing instead of what they'd been given.

This state of discontentment has the added effect of perverting our attitude about food. In their litany of complaints to Moses, the Israelites were quick to let him know what they thought of manna: "And we detest this miserable food!" (Num. 21:5). But manna wasn't miserable. Like all food, it was neutral. In truth, the problem was not the "miserable" manna at all. The problem was that their rebellious, self-indulgent hearts could not come to terms with having to live under a set of dietary restrictions. It was more convenient for them to lash out at the manna than to be introspective and repent.

I regularly experience this same attitude from people who despise the foods I recommend they eat for better health. The vegetables, fruits, and whole grains become their nemesis, and the grumbling and complaining mimics that of the Israelites: "I remember the sweet Danish rolls and bacon I once ate every morning, and now I never see anything but this oatmeal!"

Like manna, healthy foods become a convenient target. But God ordained the earth to produce foods that are beneficial to our health and well-being. How dare we complain about them? If we are discontent because of restrictions, the appropriate response is to stop complaining about the food and start examining the heart.

The issue for the Israelites was not manna but thanklessness and rebellion. Unless we are willing to let the Holy Spirit reveal our hearts, we too will respond like the Israelites and fail to address the underlying spiritual problem. Healthy foods are a blessing from God, and being content with them is "great gain." Don't allow a spirit of discontentment to cause you to despise God's gracious provisions.

Daily Prayer

Father, I rejoice today in Your provisions, and I choose to live in a state of contentment. Help me to understand that contentment brings peace and thankfulness brings joy. Lord, I purpose to take my eye off what I don't have and rejoice in what I've been given.

HEALTH FACT OF THE DAY
DAY TWENTY-SIX

Replace saturated fats with unsaturated fats in your food choices and cooking methods, and avoid trans fats to the greatest extent possible. This will help to lower your risk for heart disease.

DAY **TWENTY-SEVEN**

COUNT THE COST

And anyone who does not carry his cross and follow me
cannot be my disciple.

—LUKE 14:27

FTER JESUS SPOKE these words from Luke 14:27, He went on to give a descriptive analogy to what true discipleship required:

> Suppose one of you wants to build a tower. Will he not first sit down and estimate the cost to see if he has enough money to complete it? For if he lays the foundation and is not able to finish it, everyone who sees it will ridicule him, saying, "This fellow began to build and was not able to finish." Or suppose a king is about to go to war against another king. Will he not first sit down and consider whether he is able with ten thousand men to oppose the one coming against him with twenty thousand?
>
> —Luke 14:28–31

The reality that true discipleship carries a great cost is reflected in many of Jesus's teachings. Certainly there is a spiritual cost where our commitment to follow and obey must be our highest priority. The attributes of a true disciple are exactly what is required for making healthy lifestyle changes. A true disciple is not self-indulgent but leads a disciplined, moderate, and self-controlled life. We have examined many of these attributes, but let's now look at the concept of "counting the cost" as it pertains to practical aspects of our lives.

I believe that in most cases of weight loss failure, several issues play a role. A lack of motivation, disorganization, and inadequate knowledge all pose a threat against our success, but a major problem is when the cost was not properly counted.

130

We know food is used to meet our nourishment needs and with moderation is meant for our enjoyment. As I said before, food is a blessing from God, but it is a blessing that is sometimes abused in unhealthy, addictive ways to pacify symptoms of depression, stress, and low self-esteem. So, before starting a weight loss program, it's crucial to first determine the role that food is playing in our lives. If food has a level of significance beyond that of nourishing and healing the physical body, then part of counting the cost is to acknowledge this as a problem and then devise a strategy to resolve it. If developing a plan like this seems overwhelming, seek the help of your primary care physician, accountability partner, or counselor.

If, for instance, you eat during periods of stress, then you first need to take steps to be able to manage stress effectively *before* you begin to implement lifestyle changes. These considerations have to be done beforehand, because the things that generate stress will not change just because you decide to eat cauliflower instead of candy bars. So, part of counting the cost might include eliminating some things from your list of "things to do." Scrutinize those things that are not vitally important but that steal your time and generate stress. What tasks have you taken on that could be otherwise used for menu planning, cooking, or exercise? How many extracurricular activities are your children involved in? Are they all necessary? Do they conflict with mealtime? Scaling back to eliminate stress is part of counting the cost.

Counting the cost might require you to evaluate your relationships and accept that some of them need to change. Many times friendships are based on things that are shared in common, even if those things are superficial. Rich people tend to have rich friends. Single people often have single friends. And overweight people, quite commonly, have overweight friends. This was confirmed in a 2007 study in the *New England Journal of Medicine*, which found that a person's chances of becoming obese increased by 57 percent if he or she had a friend who became obese.[1]

When the common denominator of a relationship pertains to similar body weight, then the relationship will change if that denominator changes. In other words, if the only thing that seals the friendship is that both friends are overweight, then when one friend loses weight, the foundation is damaged and the relationship will suffer. Part of counting the cost in this scenario is first to accept that the relationship might be affected. If it is worth salvaging, then make an effort to build it on a different foundation. If it is not worth salvaging (and some are not, especially if your "friend" wants you to continue bad habits), then count the cost and accept that your friendship may dissolve.

Counting the cost must include a full understanding and an acceptance that the dietary and lifestyle changes will not be temporary but permanent. This fact is probably the most difficult part of counting the cost. It is certainly the reason why so many people regain weight after successfully losing. Then they become discouraged by their failure, and the discouragement leads to doubt. They might decide not to try again, never acknowledging that the reason for their failure was that they did not count the cost of permanent change.

Coming to terms with the end of a lifestyle is difficult—even if the lifestyle was detrimental. The old way of eating and living is gone forever, and a new lifestyle has to be learned. If there is resistance to change, then this will be a painful pill to swallow. But it is nevertheless a truth that is a necessary component of counting the cost. It has been my sad experience that sometimes a tragedy such as a heart attack or a stroke is the eye-opening event that makes a person understand that the lifestyle changes they adamantly resisted are actually beneficial.

The Bible says, "Faith by itself, if it is not accompanied by action, is dead" (James 2:17). We might have faith in our ability to change through the power of the Holy Spirit, but that faith must be accompanied by the action of counting the cost. Failure to count the cost and to work actively at overcoming those things that have kept you overweight inevitably leads to weight regain and weight cycling.

I encourage you to consider what weight loss is going to cost you. Are you prepared to pay the price? Faith alone is not enough without a willingness to accept the cost. Once that decision is made, you can expect the Lord to help you make the changes necessary for permanent weight loss to become your testimony. He is able and willing to help you overcome every obstacle that seems like a mountain in your life blocking you from achieving your goals. His grace and gentle persuasion will be your strength to equip you to live in victory for the rest of your life.

Daily Prayer

Father, I commit my life to being a disciple of Jesus Christ. I know this carries a great cost because Jesus Himself said it would. Give me the wisdom and fortitude I need to hold fast to my commitment.

HEALTH FACT OF THE DAY

DAY TWENTY-SEVEN

In a study examining the relationship between television viewing and childhood obesity, each hourly increment of television viewing by adolescents was associated with a 2 percent increase in obesity prevalence.[2]

DAY TWENTY-EIGHT

LEAVING A HEALTHY INHERITANCE FOR THE NEXT GENERATION

A good man leaves an inheritance for his children's children.
—Proverbs 13:22

THE LAW OF Moses included specific instructions regarding inheritance. Different laws applied to family members depending on the gender and birth order, with the firstborn son receiving more than the other children. Maintaining land within the family was also important because the land itself was passed on as an inheritance. The law even provided a year of jubilee when land that had been sold could be repurchased by the original family.

Along with material possessions, the father was to pass down an inheritance of virtue, teaching his children the Law of God and modeling for them, through the example of his own life, the importance of obedience. The notion of receiving an inheritance was so ingrained in the *natural* that the concept was used by David to describe his *spiritual* rewards: "The boundary lines have fallen for me in pleasant places; surely I have a delightful inheritance" (Ps. 16:6).

Most adults have an innate desire to pass on a blessing to future generations. People don't usually say, "I want my children to experience greater adversity than I did." Instead, we work hard and plan well, hoping our efforts will mean our children will be spared some of our own life's struggles.

But let's consider what we are passing on to future generations in regards to their health, a "commodity" that would be considered by many to be more precious than land or money. If we had an inheritance report card, then our grade would be an "F." Some experts predict this generation will be the first in U.S. history to have a shorter life expectancy than their parents. In terms of health, we are failing our posterity.

The reason our children will suffer with more illness upon reaching their adult years, should current trends continue, is directly related to lifestyle, specifically the way we eat (the types and amount of food) and our lack of physical activity. Consider this: the American way of living is now synonymous with poor health. When we speak of a "Western diet," or a "Western lifestyle," we aren't referring to one that is *conducive* to living scores of years with strength and vitality, but one that is *detrimental* to the health, one that will bring about disease, disability, and premature death. I consider this to be an indictment on the entire nation but especially on Christians who have specific instructions from the Bible to be mindful of future generations.

Current statistics give us evidence of how our children are suffering the consequences of improper diet and inadequate exercise with climbing rates of obesity and overweight in children and adolescents. The medical consequences, especially type 2 diabetes and cardiovascular disease, are now being detected in younger and younger age groups. Diseases that had once been the domain of the internist are being diagnosed by the pediatrician.

Certainly many things are contributing to this crisis, but I'd like to focus on just three: television viewing, eating at home, and soft drink consumption. Let the facts speak for themselves.

Television viewing

- Children from families with high television use consumed on average 5 percent more of their total daily calories from pizza, salty snacks, and soda, and 5 percent less from fruits and vegetables than did children from families with low television use.[1]
- In preschool children, the risk of obesity increases by 6 percent for every hour of television watched per day.[2]
- A child's risk for becoming obese is increased by 31 percent if there is a television in his or her bedroom.[3]
- Children aged two through eleven see on average 23 food advertisements per day, the vast majority for sugary cereal, fast food, candy, and snacks.[4]
- Television watching exposes the viewer to 8.5 to 10.3 minutes of commercials per hour, many of them for food.[5]
- African American households watch 76 hours of television per week compared to 54 hours per week in other races.[6]
- Forty percent of families either always or often watch television during dinnertime.[7]

Eating at home

- Meals eaten outside the home usually have a higher calorie and fat content than meals prepared at home.[8]
- In adolescent girls, regular family meals play a protective role against disordered eating behaviors like self-induced vomiting and the use of water pills, diet pills, and laxatives.[9]
- The more days per week children eat dinner at home, the more likely they are to have healthy eating habits.[10]
- Children who frequently eat meals with their families tend to do better in school.[11]

Soft drink consumption

- Ten to 15 percent of all calories consumed by teenaged American girls are from soft drinks.[12]
- Approximately 25 percent of adolescents drink more than 26 ounces of soda per day, which averages 12 to 15 percent of the total daily energy needs.[13]
- Soft drinks are now the leading source of added sugar in the American teenager's diet.[14]
- Every serving of sugar-sweetened beverages (soda and other sweetened drinks) is associated with an increase in the body mass index and the risk of obesity.[15]
- Approximately 60 percent of middle and high schools sell soft drinks in vending machines.[16]
- A Minnesota study found that 77 percent of their secondary schools have contracts with soft drink companies.[17]
- In reference to soft drinks, one beverage industry trade journal said, "Influencing elementary school students is very important…because children are still establishing their tastes and habits."[18]

The Book of Psalms tells us the value of children: "Sons are a heritage from the LORD, children a reward from him. Like arrows in the hands of a warrior are sons born in one's youth. Blessed is the man whose quiver is full of them. They will not be put to shame when they contend with their enemies in the gate" (Ps. 127:3–5). Our children are valuable in the sight of God. We have a responsibility to leave them an inheritance of good health.

Daily Prayer

Dear Lord, I repent for any complacency I have shown in instilling good health habits in my own children and children within my sphere of influence. I commit today to get rid of habits that are detrimental to my health and the health of my children and to teach them to honor their bodies, Your temple.

HEALTH FACT OF THE DAY
DAY TWENTY-EIGHT
In the United States, health care expenditures related to obesity and the resulting medical conditions amount to $100 billion annually.[19]

WEEKLY ASSESSMENT

My weight:	My BMI:	My waist size in inches:

I upheld my covenant by:

(Use a pencil and shade in the boxes starting from left to right to show how well you upheld your covenant this week.)

Less than 25%	25–49%	50–74%	75–99%	100%

VICTORIES: _____

_____

_____

_____

_____

_____

_____

PITFALLS: _____

_____

_____

_____

_____

_____

_____

Practice Self-Control

A WALL OF PROTECTION

*Like a city whose walls are broken down is a man
who lacks self-control.*

—PROVERBS 25:28

LIKE DAVID AND Goliath and Jonah and the fish, the Old Testament account of Joshua and the Battle of Jericho is familiar to most of us. The Bible describes Jericho as a walled city that was "tightly shut up because of the Israelites. No one went out and no one came in" (Josh. 6:1). As children, we sang songs about how Joshua fought the Battle of Jericho and the walls came down. Even beyond Sunday school classes, the account of this famous battle is a commonly used sermon topic because it is so rich in biblical principles.

Proverbs 25:28 compares a lack of self-control to an unfortified city with broken walls. Because our modern cities do not have walls, this proverb may be difficult for us to appreciate. As with many biblical passages, we need to consider the historical and cultural context before we can grasp the full impact of what God is saying. Then we can answer the question, "What is the significance of a city with broken-down walls?" and understand the comparison made to our lack of self-control.

In our era of sophisticated warfare and computer surveillance systems, it is hard to fathom the idea that a stone wall might afford much protection to a city's inhabitants or that it would represent a formidable obstacle to those who wanted to do battle with them. But that was indeed the case with ancient cities, including Jericho.

The walls surrounding the major cities of biblical times were fifteen to twenty-five feet thick and twenty-five feet high, often with observation towers built at each corner. Some walls had trenches in the front to provide additional protection. A city with a strong wall was virtually impregnable, and the inhabitants enjoyed peaceful security. If the walls of a city were compromised, the city became open to enemy attack. The land itself and everything inside the city—the money, the livestock, and the people—were vulnerable without the protection of the city wall.

The significance of the walled city in the proverb becomes clear as we understand that a lack of self-control will bring destruction to our lives just as broken walls brought destruction to a city. Self-control protects us like the ancient wall protected the city. Without it, we become vulnerable to our enemy, Satan, whose purpose is to steal, kill, and destroy (John 10:10).

It is true that the walls confined the citizens and restricted their freedom, just as self-control requires us to place restraints and limitations upon ourselves. But for the inhabitants of walled cities, the benefits of protection far exceeded the inconvenience of confinement. Such is the case with self-control. Living void of inhibitions is detrimental to our health, while practicing restraint preserves and improves our well-being. This explains why the leading cause of preventable death is related to tobacco, and the second leading cause is related to improper diet and inadequate exercise. Self-control places us in a "walled city," where we are protected from the serious, even life-threatening, consequences of an uninhibited lifestyle.

Too often, however, we have the tendency to focus on all the things we're *missing* when we practice self-control rather than all the benefits of being protected from things that can harm us. This tendency to dwell on the limitations and restrictions associated with self-control is part of human nature. We're prone to focus on the negative in every circumstance that requires us to practice restraint.

For example, God has placed the biblical requirement to practice self-control over our sexual drives. His intent is to protect us from the inevitable destruction of our lives without this restraint. People who engage in premarital sex will justify fornication based on what they're missing, failing to recognize the many benefits that come with abstaining until marriage, including protection from sexually transmitted diseases, unplanned pregnancy, and a disrupted fellowship with God because of sin.

Once our protective wall of self-control is compromised in any area, we begin a vicious cycle that leads to greater and greater damage to our already crumbling wall. The smallest crack in our wall allows Satan to enter and begin his assault. Caught off-guard, we stand vulnerable to his temptation, and the temptation is far more intense than if our wall was intact.

A small crack in the wall of self-control, for instance, might give Satan license to persuade you to venture down the snack aisle in the grocery store, the part of the store you would have otherwise avoided altogether had your wall been intact. Once in that aisle, the fissure grows wider. You find yourself putting your favorite brand of chips (which just happen to be on sale!) into your cart, promising yourself that you'll eat only a few each day. But, unbeknownst to you, the decision to purchase the chips only widened the breach, and while an intact wall would have kept you from ever entering the snack aisle, a cracked wall now places you at the cash register, purchasing what you should be avoiding. Of course, instead of keeping the few-chips-a-day commitment made in the store, you end up finishing the entire bag on the ride home.

Unfortunately, when we forfeit restraint, the wall of self-control crumbles even more, opening us up to even greater temptation. The end result is a complete disregard to practice any measure of self-control. Several years ago, an advertisement for an antacid painted the picture well. The man in need of some stomach relief lamented, "I can't believe I ate the whole thing," while his wife confirmed that he had indeed. An intact wall of self-control would have set his eating limits just to the point where his hunger was satisfied, and not beyond. But there was an obvious breach in his wall where he responded more to the tempting sight, smell, and taste of food than he did to actual hunger. With no fortified walls, this temptation proved to be more than he could handle, and he yielded and suffered the consequences.

Those with broken walls should be aware that our *natural* tendency is to give in to temptation rather than repair the breach. In the case of obesity, this evidences itself with a spirit of defeat. So, instead of gaining control, there is the downward spiral into a complete loss of control, often combined with rationalization: "Well, as heavy as I am, what difference will one more scoop of ice cream make?" And the walls come tumbling down.

Self-control is a fruit of the Spirit. As with all the fruits of the Spirit, the key to victory is learning to yield to the Holy Spirit and depend on His power within us. That is the only way to restore a wall that's been destroyed. I can do *all* things—including the extensive repairs needed for my broken down wall—through *Christ* who gives me strength! We must never believe that self-control is accomplished by means of our own willpower and determination. Spiritual maturity is manifested as we learn to rely totally upon the supernatural power that comes from the fruit of the Spirit, choosing to live in complete dependence upon Him. And then we'll experience the blessed security of living inside a fortified wall.

Daily Prayer

Father, I thank You for protecting me through the fruit of the Spirit of self-control. Please give me the desire to practice godly restraint in my eating habits so that You are glorified and my body is edified.

HEALTH FACT OF THE DAY
DAY **TWENTY-NINE**

Over the past few decades, snack food consumption has increased dramatically, now accounting for 23 percent of total calorie intake. The proportion of calories from salty snacks has doubled during this interval.[1]

DAY **THIRTY**

ACCOUNTABILITY

But the fruit of the Spirit is love, joy, peace, patience, kindness,
goodness, faithfulness, gentleness and self-control. Against such
things there is no law.

—GALATIANS 5:22–23

SELF-CONTROL IS THE only fruit of the Spirit with a bad reputation. No matter what your denominational background, the
other eight fruit listed in Galatians 5 sound pretty good. Even
an atheist or agnostic would agree that love, joy, peace, patience, kindness, goodness, faithfulness, and gentleness are character traits worth
striving for. But when it comes to self-control, our assessment is all too
often negative.

In general, we are not passionate about pursuing self-control. To the
contrary, we are inclined to ignore it, scoff at it, or be rather neutral
about it. We view self-control as a nice but unobtainable ideal that we
may speak of in theory but are incapable of practicing. These are usual
responses from non-Christians and Christians alike. The end result of
this reasoning is that instead of practicing self-control, we succumb to the
doctrine of indulgence that says, "If it feels good, do it." This attitude is
reigning supreme in the church today.

So rather than taking charge of our impulses and subduing them, we
look for "safe" ways to indulge them. "Think *before* you drink" was a
popular catchphrase for an alcoholic beverage company. But they weren't
suggesting that you seriously consider the option of not drinking at all.
I don't get the feeling that the slogan was created to encourage you to
drink in moderation, making a commitment to yourself and others to
keep things under control. Rather, the slogan serves to remind you to take
care of your business while you have the mental capacity to do so. One
should identify the designated driver and charge him with the responsibility of escorting you home in your drunken stupor *before* you take your
first sip. The unwritten message is that it is acceptable to lose control and

yield to the lusts of the flesh. What is *not* acceptable are the *consequences* of yielding—a DUI citation or a potentially fatal car accident.

We have totally rejected the notion of self-control when it comes to sexuality. Rather than exercise restraint, we encourage everyone—even children—to practice "safe" sex. The message we are sending to our youth is that the self-control abstinence requires is not a virtue God expects of His children, but it's an archaic ideal that has no place in the twenty-first century. We've shown them through example that sexual impulses ought not to be controlled but fully indulged in a "safe" manner, and that the best way to insure that everyone is "safe" is through the proper use of a condom. That way, *when* you "give in" or "yield," you'll avoid getting pregnant or catching an incurable disease (which really is a flawed assumption, since condoms do not offer 100 percent protection).

It's time for believers to reevaluate our attitude toward self-control. Self-control is one of the most profound secrets to walking in liberty from all kinds of stumbling blocks, especially the matters of overweight and obesity. The first step in maturing in the fruit of the Spirit of self-control is to accept responsibility and become accountable for your choices and actions. Simply put, it will be impossible for you to take control of a situation (i.e., your weight) if you believe the situation is hopelessly beyond your control.

The statement I frequently hear from my overweight and obese patients is that they don't eat very much. This statement might be true at the present weight because as the body weight goes up, we tend to move less and thereby expend fewer calories. So the number of calories required to *maintain* obesity is not nearly as high as the number of calories required to *become* obese. But what is vitally important to acknowledge is that the statement "I don't eat too much" *was not always the case.* If obesity is a problem, then at *some* point in your lifetime, you consumed more calories than you needed. On what evidence is this based? The BMI—an objective calculation that tells all.

Arguing against the evidence does nothing to solve the problem. Let me give a "nonmedical" example. Suppose I noticed in my garden that the plants were turning dry and brown. If I didn't know why, I might call an expert to get some advice. The master gardener would more than likely say I need to give my plants more water. Now, I could argue with him and claim that I give the plants plenty of water. I could show him my watering schedule, show him the design of my sprinkling system, and complain that he had obviously made the wrong assessment.

But the expert has nothing to gain or lose; he is only going by the evidence—the dry, brown plants. My defense of my watering practices does nothing to change the evidence. I would be better served (and my plants would be better served) if I became less defensive and accepted personal responsibility for the state of my garden. Maybe I'm *not* giving an adequate amount, or maybe I'm watering at the wrong time of day and much of the water is evaporating, or maybe I need to amend my soil so that it will absorb the water more effectively. Whatever the case, I cannot solve the problem until I accept responsibility and become accountable to the expert.

One of the reasons people struggle to lose weight and avoid taking responsibility for being overweight is that they became overweight during childhood (or even during the infant or toddler years). They *didn't* have full control of their eating, and they *aren't* responsible for the poor habits established by their parents or caretakers. Now their bodies have an established "set point," and they are extremely efficient at conserving calories. Weight loss is very difficult, seemingly impossible.

In this case, it is important to acknowledge the actions of others and accept that their decisions contributed to your problem. In order for you to reverse the results of their actions in your past, however, you will have to assume responsibility for your present and future. You are now responsible for *un*doing (to the best of your ability) the mistakes your parents made. It will be *your* responsibility to engage in regular exercise to improve your metabolism and break those weight plateaus, and *you* will be responsible for changing those unhealthy eating habits that were established during your childhood.

Whatever the root of the problem, your role now is to become accountable and accept responsibility to develop the fruit of self-control. As you allow the Holy Spirit to work in your life, you will find the strength to make right choices and become responsible for your actions.

Daily Prayer

Lord, I am grateful for the fruit of the Spirit of self-control. Now I ask that You show me areas in my life where repentance is in order. Reveal to me where I have blamed others or walked in denial. I know these tendencies will prevent me from taking responsibility for my actions, and that will in turn hinder my ability to change.

HEALTH FACT OF THE DAY

DAY THIRTY

A 2006 study showed that only 36 percent of parents with overweight children, or children at risk for being overweight, described their child as "overweight" or "a little overweight." The researchers concluded that many parents may not be able to identify if their child is at risk for obesity and its related medical problems.[1]

GET A HOLD OF YOURSELF

I can do everything through him who gives me strength.
—Philippians 4:13

THERE IS ABUNDANT evidence that genetics play a role in body weight and that the tendency toward obesity can be inherited. Adoption studies have shown that children whose biological parents were overweight have a higher than average likelihood of being overweight themselves, no matter what their adoptive parents weigh. So even if you have started eating a healthier diet and exercising regularly, if Grandpa, Grandma, Mom, Dad, and all your siblings are obese, you undoubtedly have a strong genetic component that is going to work against you.

This may be one reality, but it is reassuring to know that DNA is not able to nullify the first law of thermodynamics. For those who never took physics (and for all those who took it but forgot the principles after the final exam), let me give a quick lesson: *For any process, the difference between the heat supplied to the system and the work done by the system equals the change in the internal energy.*

Don't be intimidated by the technical jargon. For our purposes, this law applies to the reality that the calories we consume in the form of food are either burned or stored. This basic law guarantees that if we eat and absorb into our systems more calories than we utilize, those extra calories will not just disappear, but will be stored in the form of fat. We utilize calories through our bodies' normal functions—functions like a beating heart, a thinking brain, and a churning stomach—and through the voluntary and involuntary use of our muscles. Of course, our muscles use calories when we engage in regular exercise. But even when we aren't active, our muscles still require a certain amount of energy to maintain posture and tone.

The obvious conclusion to the first law of thermodynamics as it relates to body weight is that if we consistently consume more calories than we burn, the extra calories will lead to weight gain. If, however, we

149

consistently eat *fewer* calories than what our bodies require, the additional calories that we need will (ideally) come from that unused energy previously stored in the form of fat. I qualify this last statement with "ideally" because when we approach weight loss in the wrong manner, it is possible for those additional calories to come from our lean muscle tissue and not our fat stores.

Yes, genetics play a role in determining our body frame. But our genes do not nullify the first law of thermodynamics, and intuitively we all know this to be true. Imagine, for example, that an obese person was stranded on a deserted island where the only foods available to eat were low in calories but rich in nutrients. And imagine that this food was only obtained after working hard for several hours each day. And suppose that, despite our island dweller's best efforts, there was a limit to the quantity of food he could eat each day, and that quantity was about eighteen hundred calories. In this hypothetical situation, it would not matter if every member of our castaway's family were obese; he would eventually lose weight.

This is because genes don't override the first law of thermodynamics. The fairly recent increase in the prevalence of obesity bears witness to this. Our genes have not changed significantly over the past couple of generations, but the incidence of obesity has skyrocketed. The upward trend in our bodyweight over a few decades reflects the effect of lifestyle to a greater extent than genetics.

But we live in an era when blame is a way of life. Looking for an outside force at which to point our finger has become par for the course, even when our circumstances are within our control. DNA has become the latest entity to bear the brunt of our accusations. Keep in mind, the tendency to blame is tightly linked to the mind-set of a victim, and the victim mentality is detrimental to our health.

We have become so comfortable with being victims that what is required for true victorious living is now unacceptable to many Christians. Victorious living requires self-control, which is an attribute of the Holy Spirit. If we abandon self-control, then the mind-set of the victim will soon follow, not only in our eating but also in every area of our lives. Sure, we sing songs that speak of our victory in Christ, but when it comes to actually experiencing this victory in our everyday lives—experience which comes by way of denying the flesh—we're missing the mark.

We can't live victoriously in the area of our health until we choose to take control of our lifestyles—control over what we eat, how much we eat, and our activity level. But weight loss is only a small part of what we are missing. We won't know the victory that comes through forgiving those who have hurt us until we take control of our emotional response. We won't know the victory of sexual purity until we gain control of our carnal nature. And we won't know the victory in financial freedom until we get a handle on self-indulgent spending. The list goes on and on.

Are you a victim or a victor? Let the evidence speak for itself. The question to ask is this: "Am I powerless in this situation?" Your answer reveals whether your mind-set is that of a victim or a victor. The victor knows the Holy Spirit gives us power to live a life that reflects the discipline, moderation, self-denial, and self-control found in Jesus Christ. The person with a victim mentality, however, resigns himself to the thought that his condition and circumstances are beyond his control and—worse yet—beyond the help of God. He does not believe that changing his lifestyle is possible, so he is comfortable with yielding to temptation and submitting to the cravings of the flesh. The negative consequences that follow only fuel this sense of helplessness.

I don't want to be misunderstood. I am not implying that bad things only happen to people with a victim mentality. Obviously that is not the case. Bad things happen to all types of people, and many times we are confronted with health challenges that are well beyond our control. But the victim has a fatalistic attitude about everything, and he will not try to change even those things that are within his control.

The difference between the victim and the victor lies in the way they approach circumstances, those that are changeable and those that are unchangeable. The victim will make no effort to change a potentially alterable set of circumstances, while the victor will challenge his or her situation. When the circumstances are *unchangeable*, the victim will wallow in self-pity while the victor will rise above them.

Through the power of the Holy Spirit, we *can* live victoriously. Don't deny the work of the cross in your day-to-day living. Instead, keep our daily verse at the forefront of your mind. You *have* the strength through Jesus Christ to take control of your lifestyle and improve your health.

Daily Prayer

Lord, I thank You for giving me a free will, and I thank You also for giving me wisdom in making choices that pertain to my health. I ask according to Your Word that You give me the strength through Jesus Christ to lead a lifestyle that is pleasing to You.

HEALTH FACT OF THE DAY
DAY **THIRTY-ONE**

According to a British study, the risk of ten different cancers increases as body mass index rises. The association was found in endometrial, kidney, ovarian, colorectal, pancreatic, esophageal, and breast cancer, as well as leukemia, multiple myeloma, and non-Hodgkin's lymphoma.[1]

WE EAT TOO MUCH

*Keep falsehood and lies far from me; give me neither poverty nor
riches, but give me only my daily bread. Otherwise, I may have too
much and disown you and say, "Who is the LORD?" Or I may
become poor and steal, and so dishonor the name of my God.*

—PROVERBS 30:8–9

GOOD EATING HABITS are reflected in both the quality and the quantity of food. In terms of quality, we want our food to provide nutrients that will promote health and protect against disease. Some foods give us energy but have a low nutritional value. We call the calories they provide "empty." These foods are not beneficial to our health, and some might even be harmful.

Our goal is to select foods that are edifying and to avoid or minimize our consumption of foods that offer no nutritional benefit. But as I have already said, weight gain results from too many calories, irrespective of the quality of the food. Put another way, it's altogether possible to have "too much of a good thing." Yes, overeating low-quality food leads to weight gain, but so does overeating high-quality food. In terms of weight gain, food quality is not as big an issue as is net calories. Don't fall into the erroneous mind-set that healthy foods are exempt from quantity restriction.

Our calorie requirements are related to our metabolic needs. Our metabolic needs factor in several parameters including age, gender, and activity level. So, what may be an appropriate amount of food for a lean adolescent boy who plays sports and is in the middle of a growth spurt would be entirely *inappropriate* for a middle-aged woman who sits at a desk all day and never exercises. It is imperative that we understand our caloric needs and practice self-control in meeting those needs.

I am not an advocate of severely structured diet plans, the types that tell you exactly what to eat for every meal, each day of the week. I think that eating should have some level of spontaneity and flexibility, but I do find structured diet plans particularly helpful when I meet men and

153

women who insist they don't overeat despite progressive weight gain. Using a sample diet brings much-needed objectivity to their assessments.

Below is a sample menu for breakfast, lunch, dinner, and a snack from a 1,600-calorie diet plan. Pay particular attention to the serving sizes (the *quantity* of food) and the relative absence of foods that are comprised of empty calories (the *quality* of food).

Breakfast
1 cup oatmeal
½ cup fruit
1 cup plain, low-fat yogurt
Black coffee or tea with lemon

Lunch
2 slices whole-wheat bread
2 oz. turkey or ham and 1 oz. low-fat cheese
¼ avocado sliced
Alfalfa sprouts
1 tsp. mayonnaise
½ cup baby carrots
2 tablespoons nonfat dressing for dipping carrots
1 apple
Water or non-caloric beverage

Dinner
5 oz. chicken leg, no skin, baked
1 cup whole-wheat pasta
4 Tbsp. low-fat vinaigrette (2 Tbsp. for marinade for chicken and 2 Tbsp. to toss with pasta)
1 cup broccoli and 1 cup zucchini, steamed and tossed with pasta
8 oz. skim milk

Snack
1 cup cantaloupe
¼ cup 1% cottage cheese

Most of my patients who review this typical 1,600-calorie menu are amazed at the difference between the amount of food they *should* be eating and what they actually eat. Even the foods that are nutritionally sound are restricted in terms of quantity. Notice, for instance, the breakfast meal has *one* cup of oatmeal, not two. And the meat allowed with dinner is one small, skinless, baked chicken leg—not three large pieces fried extra crispy and drenched with barbeque sauce.

This sample diet also reveals how empty calories are a major problem. Where are the chips, candy, cookies, ice cream, and soft drinks in this 1,600-calorie menu? They aren't included because once the daily nutritional needs are met, there is not much room left to allow for empty calories.

Beverage calories deserve special attention. Notice in our sample menu, the only beverage calories were found in the milk served at dinnertime, a total of 90 calories. So our menu allows for beverages to comprise only about 6 percent of the daily calories. But suppose we selected—as many who say they want to lose weight do—a 12 oz. can of soda for our lunch and also dinner. With each can containing 150 empty calories, we would consume a total of 300 beverage calories per day, or close to 20 percent of the 1,600 total calories. Of course if you drank a 20-ounce bottle instead, the calories consumed would be even greater.

To make matters worse, liquid calories do not satisfy hunger in the same way that solid foods do. So we end up consuming a lot of calories having no nutritional value, and we're still left feeling hungry.

Ideally, the calories we take in should satisfy our hunger. But liquid calories do not do this especially well. This is why we must also reconsider the role of fruit juices in our diets. Yes, the juice has more nutritional value than a can of soda, but it still provides calories in the form of liquid, which won't relieve hunger very well. For weight loss, you are better off drinking water and eating a piece of fruit than drinking fruit juice. The water will quench your thirst, and the substance of the fruit (especially the fiber) will satisfy your hunger.

The 1,600-calorie menu plan is eye opening mainly because it reveals our own role in our weight. The truth of the matter is that in order to live a life governed by self-control, we must be willing to hold ourselves accountable for our choices and accept responsibility for our actions. The sample menu proves that many of us just eat too much! And until we are willing to come to terms with that truth and go about changing it, we will not know success.

But accepting the truth is hard for some. I remember one patient I cared for years ago who was dealing with obesity and finding it hard to control type 2 diabetes. Every visit, after being weighed by the nurse, she'd shrug her shoulders and shake her head in frustration. Her weight was predictably a pound or two more than it was on our previous visit, but she was adamant in her stance that it was not her fault.

One day while I was rushing to the clinic, I passed by the hospital's gift shop at the same time that she was exiting, and we nearly collided with one another. Her mouth was so completely stuffed with candy that I could hardly understand her when she greeted me. She didn't even wait to get out of the store before she started eating! I smiled and returned her greeting, but we gave one another a look that confirmed her secret: the mystery weight gain was really no mystery at all. The greater mystery was why she refused to take any responsibility for her actions.

The prophet Hosea gave the warning, "My people are destroyed from lack of knowledge" (Hos. 4:6). Though we have much knowledge about how we can improve our health, we are still being destroyed by diseases that are modifiable by lifestyle. We are suffering because we have avoided the crucial step of accepting responsibility and being accountable. When we face up to our actions, we will no longer maintain the stance of hapless victims, but we will instead experience victory through improving our health.

Daily Prayer

Heavenly Father, help me to accept that my actions and inaction have played a role in my weight and health. Help me to see that change will only come when I accept responsibility for my own decisions. I am grateful for Your wisdom and power as I make a fresh commitment to take better care of my body, Your temple.

HEALTH FACT OF THE DAY
DAY THIRTY-TWO

Insoluble and soluble fiber are beneficial to the health in ways other than reducing constipation. They reduce the risk of cardiovascular disease by helping to lower serum cholesterol, lower blood pressure, and improve the metabolism of glucose (blood sugar).

UNCONTROLLED IMPULSES

Everyone who competes in the games goes into strict training.
They do it to get a crown that will not last; but we do it to get a
crown that will last forever. Therefore I do not run like a man running
aimlessly; I do not fight like a man beating the air. No, I beat my body
and make it my slave so that after I have preached to others, I myself
will not be disqualified for the prize.

—1 CORINTHIANS 9:25–27

WHEN WE CONSIDER self-control, one way to gauge ourselves is to examine how we handle impulses. Keep in mind, the biblical precepts we are examining in reference to weight loss are not specific to eating and exercise habits but should be applied to all areas of our lives. Certainly, impulse eating presents a serious problem, but another area where our impulses can get us into big trouble is when it comes to money.

At this writing, the United States is in the middle of a foreclosure crisis where, in some states, more than one out of every four hundred homes is facing foreclosure. Of course, there are many reasons for this, but we can't ignore one common denominator—unrestrained impulses. Some folks were driven by impulse to buy more house than they could actually afford. This same impulse also drives people to eat more than they should.

Most of the principles pertaining to "capital stewardship" are equally relevant when it comes to "temple stewardship." The problem with uncontrolled impulses is that they can wreak havoc not only in our wallets but also on our health. Unless we subject the flesh to the point where our impulses, as the apostle Paul would say, are beaten down and made our slaves, then we won't know victory.

There are many wonderful Christian organizations that provide financial advice to help men and women understand the way God expects us to handle money, but I am going to take these same principles and refocus them on our health.

1. Stewardship

The most important concept to learn—a concept many never fully appreciate—is that "our" resources are not ours at all. Everything belongs to God; we are just His stewards, which is another term for "manager." In the Book of Deuteronomy, the Israelites are warned about the tendency to forget the source of their blessings. Moses tells them, "You may say to yourself, 'My power and the strength of my hands have produced this wealth for me.' But remember the LORD your God, for it is he who gives you the ability to produce wealth, and so confirms his covenant, which he swore to your forefathers, as it is today" (Deut. 8:17–18). Our money belongs to the Lord; we are required to be faithful managers.

Likewise, the Bible tells us our bodies are not our own, but they belong to God: "Do you not know that your body is a temple of the Holy Spirit, who is in you, whom you have received from God? *You are not your own; you were bought at a price.* Therefore honor God with your body" (1 Cor. 6:19–20, emphasis added).

A faithful steward, whether taking care of God's money or God's temple, understands that *personal* desires are not part of the plan. The good manager will diligently seek and adhere to whatever it is that the *owner* desires. If his or her personal desires fail to line up with the owner's desires, then it is the *personal* desires that are relinquished.

2. Discerning needs vs. wants

A sure way to get into financial trouble is through misunderstanding the difference between a "need" and a "want." In general, impulse spending is for things we want. We see it, we fall for the persuasive advertising, we convince ourselves we can't live without it, and then we buy it without taking thought of the cost or the consequences.

The sad truth is that many people refuse to accept that *needs* take precedence over *wants*. What frequently happens is that their "needs" are compromised because they have misappropriated their resources toward satisfying "wants." So they fall behind in the rent or mortgage payments or have inadequate insurance coverage yet maintain a closet full of designer originals.

When it comes to temple stewardship, this same phenomenon exists. We *want* so many foods that we ought to restrict or avoid, and then we avoid the kinds of foods our bodies truly *need*. Clearly, if our impulses are left unchecked, we set ourselves up for becoming sick and poor.

3. Proper planning

In the area of finances, planning requires a budget. In the area of weight control, planning requires a menu. When we utilize a budget, we are able to see our income and expenses clearly and then balance them. We can then be proactive, using wisdom with planned spending rather than speculation and assumption. A budget provides parameters and restraint. If we don't have one, we are prone to lose control and spend money impulsively. Interestingly enough, despite the proven benefits of following a budget, most people don't use them.

Likewise, a menu is crucial to good eating habits. But I find that many people who are overweight or obese or have medical conditions influenced by diet do surprisingly little meal planning. Trying to manage money is difficult without a budget, and trying to eat a nutritionally sound, calorie-appropriate diet is difficult without a menu or some form of meal planning. When we fail to plan, we are prone to eat whatever is available, and that often means fast food, junk food, or highly processed meals that are high in sodium and calories.

4. Discipline

Discipline is vitally important both to temple stewardship and capital stewardship. Without discipline, both our spending habits and our eating habits tend to become erratic and excessive. And without discipline, both the practice of saving and investing and the practice of regular exercise fall by the wayside.

Believers are indwelt by the Holy Spirit, whose very character is that of self-control. If yielding to impulses has prevented you from making lifestyle changes to improve your health (or your finances), then please understand that God has equipped you through the power of the Holy Spirit to lead a self-controlled life. Reflect on this truth, and manifest it in your daily living. Don't, as the apostle Paul warned, become "disqualified for the prize" because of uncontrolled impulses.

Daily Prayer

Lord, I thank You for giving me the capacity to subject my flesh. I know that Your desire for me is to live by the Spirit and not gratify the desires of the flesh. In all areas of my life, help me to take authority over my impulses rather than being controlled by them.

HEALTH FACT OF THE DAY

DAY THIRTY-THREE

Since 1970, the prevalence of overweight children between the ages of two and five years old has doubled, and that of children and teens between the ages of six and nineteen years old has tripled.[1]

THE NATURE OF TEMPTATION

Now the serpent was more crafty than any of the wild animals
the LORD God had made.

—GENESIS 3:1

WHEN IT COMES to temptation, I have good news and bad news. The good news first: through the power of the Holy Spirit, we do not have to yield to temptation—ever! Promise after promise in Scripture reminds us of how wonderfully prepared we are when it comes to standing against the power of temptation.

The Bible tells us God is able to rescue us when confronted:

> The Lord knows how to rescue godly men from trials.
>
> —2 Peter 2:9

Jesus gives us solid advice on preventing a fall:

> Watch and pray so that you will not fall into temptation.
>
> —Matthew 26:41

And we're even given specific instruction on what to do in order to prevail:

> Submit yourselves, then, to God. Resist the devil, and he will
> flee from you.
>
> —James 4:7

Now the bad news: we still fall—all the time. For many, the inability to follow a healthy lifestyle rests entirely on the matter of temptation. I believe the reason Christians fall (despite being equipped to stand) is that we neither understand the nature of temptation, nor do we appreciate its power.

As any soldier knows, when you fail to appreciate your enemy's strategy, you've positioned yourself for defeat—even when you are the stronger opponent. Keep in mind, temptation has proven to be a highly effective method that Satan has employed since the dawn of mankind. We'd do well to be "as shrewd as serpents" in our approach to it.

The account of Creation is found in the first two chapters of the Book of Genesis. On the sixth day, God created man in His image. While all creation was special—whether land, water, vegetation, or animal—man alone was given the unique attribute of being created in God's image. (See Genesis 1:27.)

This status carried with it the responsibility of subduing the earth and taking authority over other living things. Along with having dominion over the earth, man was also given the unique ability to make choices. Unlike the animal kingdom, we do not operate by instinct but by our decision-making capacity. Complete freedom of choice sets us apart from other living things but carries with it a great risk—that of making the wrong choice. Since temptation's slippery slope rests upon our privilege to choose, it is this blessing of free will that ultimately makes us vulnerable to the power of temptation.

Before the first sin, mankind enjoyed a special relationship with God where fellowship was open and communion was not hindered by rebellion. Adam, the first man, was commissioned by God to care for the Garden of Eden. In His instructions, God allowed him to exercise his free will. Interestingly enough, the first set of options presented to Adam pertained to eating:

> And the LORD God commanded the man, "You are free to eat
> from any tree in the garden; but you must not eat from the
> tree of the knowledge of good and evil, for when you eat of it
> you will surely die."
>
> —Genesis 2:16–17

Adam, then, had the choice to eat what was approved (and there was plenty of it) or to eat that which was forbidden. God gave a command and did not hedge in describing the consequences for violating the command. The words "when you eat of it you will surely die" leave little room for speculation.

In the serpent's dialogue with Eve, he twisted the truth with his first inquiry. Instead of resisting the devil by reflecting on God's actual words—words that would have reminded her of the Father's abundant provisions—Eve chose to engage in a conversation with the enemy.

Satan's first lie led to others, and Eve soon found herself yielding to the devil's temptation. With this fall, sin entered the world. Keep in mind the temptation itself did not lead to the fall of mankind—yielding to it did. Being subjected to temptation is not a sin; it is an unavoidable part of life. What we must learn to do is resist that which we cannot avoid.

I find it interesting that food was the thing used to tempt Adam and Eve to commit the original sin. Of the many ways they could have rebelled against God and opened the door for sin to enter the world, getting them to eat what they shouldn't have eaten, when there were other more acceptable things available to eat, was Satan's method of choice. Then and now, food is an irresistible enticement.

However, we know that God intended food to be a blessing. God gives food for our nourishment, enjoyment, and as a means for fellowship. He designed the earth to produce a wide variety of foods to meet every nutritional need, at every stage of life. God blessed man by giving him dominion over the earth and access to its abundant supply of fruits, grains, vegetables, and animals for our sustenance, growth, and strength. In His great love, He made eating enjoyable with tastes, textures, and smells that are pleasant.

Every civilization throughout the history of mankind has used food to facilitate fellowship and enhance relationships. A meal shared will strengthen the ties uniting families, friends, and neighbors. A shared meal can even be a conduit for reconciliation to those who are estranged. The early church was characterized by regular mealtime fellowship: "They broke bread in their homes and ate together with glad and sincere hearts, praising God and enjoying the favor of all the people" (Acts 2:46–47).

Everything that God intends to be a blessing, Satan sets out to pervert—and food is no exception. The devil confounds us to such an extent that we often cannot detect temptation, even in the process of yielding.

I have a friend who shared an eye-opening experience with me where she saw firsthand how temptation clouds our thinking. Her weakness is fast food, and she tends to order the extra-large servings of french fries and beverages, justifying it as a good value. She told me that once, after sitting down with her meal, she bowed her head to say a prayer of thanksgiving. As she started to pray, she had the unmistakable feeling that she was grieving the Holy Spirit. She sat still for a moment and then received insight from God on her behavior. "All along I had been thanking God before I indulged myself and yielded to temptation," she told me. "But God made things clear to me that afternoon. He wanted me to see what I was doing. I was actually thanking Him for what He was opposed to."

She went on to relate how jolted she was upon recognizing that she was actually *thanking* God for the opportunity and the means to yield to temptation. It was like Eve thanking God before biting the forbidden fruit—the fruit He said would make her "surely die." My friend acknowledged her error and saw just how tricky temptation can be. She was deceived to the extent that she failed to discern how the devil used food as a tool to damage her health.

While God gives food for our edification and enjoyment, Satan uses it for destruction. Nothing good comes from yielding to temptation—no matter what the source of the temptation. Our health can be harmed by the many diseases related to the types of foods we eat and excessive body weight. And beyond our physical well-being, yielding to temptation will plant the seeds for such harmful emotions as shame, guilt, and regret.

As long as we live, we will find ourselves surrounded by temptation. That's the nature of the world. But we can rejoice and be exceedingly glad that our heavenly Father has equipped us to resist!

Daily Prayer

> *Lord, I am thankful for what Your death and resurrection accomplished. Through my faith in You, the devil has now become a defeated foe. Please keep me mindful of his plan to destroy my health and even to kill my physical body by using what You have given to me as a blessing. Give me discernment to see his malicious plans, and help me to understand that when I submit to You and resist him, he will have to flee.*

HEALTH FACT OF THE DAY
DAY THIRTY-FOUR

There is evidence that obesity and being overweight is associated with the development of asthma, with girls and women carrying a higher risk than men. The reason for the association is not understood and may be related to the influence of hormones, genetic factors, or possibly gastroesophageal reflux disease. Whatever the mechanism, weight reduction can result in improvement of lung function.

DAY *THIRTY-FIVE*

FASTING AND PRAYER

And when you pray, do not be like the hypocrites for they love
to pray standing in the synagogues and on the street corners to be seen
by men. I tell you the truth, they have received their reward in full....
When you fast, do not look somber as the hypocrites do, for
they disfigure their faces to show men they are fasting. I tell you the
truth, they have received their reward in full.

—MATTHEW 6:5, 16

ANY CHRISTIAN WHO is trying to lose weight must make fasting and prayer regular practices for life. Fasting and prayer keep us connected with God, the source of our strength. When we fast and pray, we maintain an intimate relationship with God. We know that He alone is the source of our strength, and He is the One who gives us power to live by the Spirit in victory over sin.

It is important that we understand these disciplines in order to reap their benefits. A patient once told me that her daily prayer was for God to completely remove her craving for sweets. I advised her not to hold her breath waiting. God has never promised to eliminate the many challenges of life. If the Spirit Himself led Jesus Christ into the wilderness to be tempted by the devil, then we should hardly expect to be exempt from the same.

A commitment to fasting and prayer requires a tremendous amount of self-discipline and self-control. Giving these redemptive graces a high priority in our busy lives requires discipline; maintaining our focus during prayer and staying committed to a fast require self-control.

In the ninth chapter of the Gospel of Mark, we're given the account of Jesus's transfiguration. The latter part of this chapter tells us what happened when He and three of His disciples—Peter, James, and John—came down from the mountain where He was transfigured. As they approached the crowds, an unidentified man knelt before Christ and asked that He heal his son. The man described the illness and added that Jesus's other disciples had tried, but they were unable to heal the boy. Jesus then healed the child in the presence of His disciples as well as a large crowd of scribes and onlookers.

Later, in a private meeting, His disciples asked Jesus why they were unsuccessful in bringing healing to the boy. Jesus responded, "This kind cannot be driven out by anything but prayer and fasting" (Mark 9:29, AMP). Some problems can't be solved without tapping into the power of God through prayer and fasting. When we make these disciplines a regular part of our lives, God has promised that He will answer us and give us whatever we need to meet the challenges that face us.

Prayer accomplishes many things. It's a time to praise God; it's a time to ask God for wisdom and provisions; it's a time to thank God; and it's a time to intercede on behalf of others. But when we set out to make lifestyle changes for weight loss and better health, one vitally important purpose for prayer cannot be overlooked: prayer is a time to confess sin.

When we make the commitment to seek God's help in overcoming obesity, the first and crucial step is the confession of any sin that has contributed to the obesity, which may include the sins of idolatry and gluttony. According to Scripture, gluttony is a sin. It is included along with drunkenness in passages from Deuteronomy, Proverbs, Matthew, and Luke. When we yield to the desires of our flesh by indulging ourselves in excessive amounts of food, we commit the sin of gluttony.

Fasting and prayer provide us the opportunity to draw closer to God and repent of anything that hinders our fellowship with Him. After confession of sin comes repentance. Repentance means that we agree with God that our behavior is wrong, and then we choose to turn away from it. We don't justify in true repentance; we agree. We don't blame in true repentance; we agree. We don't rationalize or make excuses in true repentance; we agree.

Christians have become so comfortable with the grace and mercy of God that we are prone to forget how offensive sinfulness is to Him. When we repent during a fast, our hunger and weakness serve to reinforce our feelings of contrition and remind us of how totally dependent we are on the very God that we've offended. Yet we know that He is faithful to forgive us of sin that we confess.

A spiritual fast is *not* a method for losing weight! We don't engage in a fast for the purpose of gaining a boost in our weight loss efforts. Just as praise dancing is not aerobic exercise, so spiritual fasting in not a way to jump-start a weight loss plan. We don't "prepare" to fast by engorging ourselves with several days' worth of food prior to starting. Binge eating is not the type of activity that is conducive to fellowship with

God. Likewise, we ought not to begin a fast with our minds preoccupied by thoughts of when our fast will end. How can we commune with God when we're distracted by counting the hours (even the minutes) until we're "permitted" to satisfy our flesh?

A fast is a time to turn down the plate for the purpose of drawing closer to God. If we start tallying the number of extra calories that will be burned in the process, the focus is taken completely off God and placed entirely on self. The fast then becomes an exercise motivated by selfishness rather than a time of seeking God's face for meaningful fellowship.

When spiritual acts are performed out of self-centeredness, they become useless rituals. Whatever is accomplished is minimal and insignificant. Our verse today is taken from Matthew 6, where Jesus teaches about fasting and prayer. He mentions the religious hypocrites who fasted and prayed in order to draw attention to themselves and receive accolades from other less religious people. They did receive a reward in full—the recognition from those who were impressed by their "holiness." They missed the greater reward of recognition from God, who knew their hearts and knew their true motivation.

When a fast is motivated by personal gain, then the benefits will be small, just as they were for the hypocritical religious leaders. You will burn up a few hundred calories but miss the greater reward of hearing from God, repenting from sin, and growing stronger in faith and self-control. The calories burned in a selfishly motivated fast will accumulate after one visit to the ice cream parlor, but a fast done with the proper motivation will change your life.

Prayer and fasting are practices that will facilitate our hearing from God as He reveals to us those things we need to change. When done with a pure heart and the right motivation, they allow us to receive from God the power to implement the change.

Daily Prayer

Thank You, God, for the example set by Jesus Christ on the power of fasting and prayer. It is a blessing and a privilege to come to Your throne of grace, presenting my needs to my loving Father. I ask that You create a clean heart within me as I make changes in my lifestyle for better health.

HEALTH FACT OF THE DAY

DAY THIRTY-FIVE

People who eat a healthy breakfast on a regular basis are less likely to become obese.

WEEKLY ASSESSMENT

My weight:	My BMI:	My waist size in inches:

I upheld my covenant by:

(Use a pencil and shade in the boxes starting from left to right to show how well you upheld your covenant this week.)

Less than 25%	25–49%	50–74%	75–99%	100%

VICTORIES: _____

_____

_____

_____

_____

_____

_____

_____

PITFALLS: _____

_____

_____

_____

_____

_____

_____

_____

The Practical and the Spiritual

BODY FAT DISTRIBUTION

*Please test your servants for ten days: Give us nothing but
vegetables to eat and water to drink....At the end of the ten
days they looked healthier and better nourished than any of
the young men who ate the royal food.*

—DANIEL 1:12, 15

BODY FAT DISTRIBUTION plays such an important role in health that many clinicians advocate using the waist circumference (which reflects the distribution of fat) in combination with the BMI (which reflects the absolute weight) when assessing a person's risk for cardiovascular disease and type 2 diabetes. This is because abdominal fat, also called "central obesity," "upper body obesity," or "truncal obesity," has metabolic consequences that are more striking than when the fat is located peripherally—predominantly on the hips and thighs. In very simplistic terms, abdominal fat is inside the body cavity while peripheral fat is just under the skin.

Being overweight or obese is not good, but the health consequences vary with the shape, even when the weight is constant. In other words, if two people weigh exactly the same amount, the person with the "apple" shape will have a higher risk for cardiovascular disease than the person with the "pear" shape.

Body fat distribution is assessed most easily in an office setting by measuring the waist circumference, or the waist-to-hip ratio (the waist measurement divided by the hip measurement). Some studies show the waist measurement alone is better at predicting the risk for cardiovascular disease than the waist-to-hip ratio; however, a recent study showed a parallel association between the waist-to-hip ratio and mortality in middle-aged women.[1] A waist-to-hip ratio of less than 0.95 for men and 0.8 for women is desirable. For waist circumference, a measurement of greater than 40 inches in men or 35 inches in women increases risk.

The waist measurement is included in the criteria for the metabolic syndrome, which is a set of health risk factors that are associated with an increased chance for developing such conditions as heart disease, peripheral vascular disease, stroke, and diabetes. The syndrome is confirmed if three or more of the following five criteria are met:

Criteria	Defining Level
Abdominal obesity, waist circumference in inches	Men > 40 in
	Women > 35 in
Triglycerides	> 150 mg/dl
HDL cholesterol	Men < 40 mg/dl
	Women < 50 mg/dl
Blood pressure	> 130/85
Fasting glucose	> 100 mg/dl

Three of the criteria (triglycerides, HDL cholesterol, and fasting glucose) are determined by blood tests; the other two by simple measurements that can be taken in or outside your doctor's office.

It is currently estimated that fifty million American adults have the metabolic syndrome. The definition for metabolic syndrome in children is not as clear-cut, although studies show that children who meet the criteria set for adults are more likely to develop cardiovascular disease and diabetes during their adult years. There are racial and gender differences in the syndrome as well. Hispanics, for instance, have a 32 percent prevalence rate compared to the 24 percent prevalence in the general population, and African American women have a higher prevalence than African American men.[2]

Several factors contribute to the development of the metabolic syndrome, including genetics, being overweight, and being physically inactive. Recent studies also link the quality of the diet to the development of the syndrome. The typical Western diet—one high in meat, refined grains, fried foods, and soda (including diet soda)—increases the chance of developing the metabolic syndrome,[3] while a Mediterranean diet is likely protective.

So, changing our eating habits for better health requires a two-pronged approach: cutting the number of calories consumed will affect the BMI, but changing the types of foods eaten will affect the body fat distribution. Both quality and quantity are important for our total health.

Daily Prayer

Lord, I thank You for the fearful and wonderful way You have created me. I recognize that disease entered the world with the fall of mankind, but I rejoice in Your faithfulness. You have provided us with knowledge on how to protect our health against unnecessary destruction to preserve our lives according to Your will.

HEALTH FACT OF THE DAY
DAY THIRTY-SIX

Physical or mental stress causes the release of norepinephrine and glucocorticoids from the sympathetic nervous system. These substances cause elevations in the blood glucose and trigger inflammation and may thereby contribute to the development of the metabolic syndrome.[4]

TRANS FATS

*He waters the mountains from his upper chambers; the earth is
satisfied by the fruit of his work. He makes grass grow for the cattle,
and plants for man to cultivate—bringing forth food from the earth:
wine that gladdens the heart of man, oil to make his face shine, and
bread that sustains his heart.*

—Psalm 104:13–15

TRANS FATS HAVE received much media attention in recent years, and for good reason. I like to think of them as a testimony that tampering with the natural state of food may not be such a good idea. While miniscule amounts of trans fats occur naturally in meats and dairy products from cows and sheep, the majority of trans fats in our diet are produced through the process of partial hydrogenation.

Animal fats are semisolid at room temperature while vegetable fat is liquid (oil). The partial hydrogenation process introduces hydrogen into vegetable oil, and this converts the liquid into a semisolid fat, which is used in baking and frying. So semisolid, partially hydrogenated vegetable oils are where we find trans fats. Major sources are bakery products, deep-fried fast foods, crackers, packaged snack foods, and margarine.

From a cardiovascular standpoint, trans fats are more harmful than even saturated fat. While saturated fat will elevate the LDL (bad) cholesterol, trans fat elevates both the LDL cholesterol as well as the triglycerides, and it also lowers the level of HDL (good) cholesterol. Since trans fats, unlike cholesterol, are not an animal product, it is entirely possible to strictly avoid cholesterol and still eat foods that adversely affect the cholesterol level.

I recall a patient whose cholesterol was elevated to the point that I wanted to begin medications. He was not happy about this and asked that we allow a few months for him to modify his diet, to which I agreed. When we repeated his lipid panel a few months later, his numbers were even worse, despite the fact that he had dramatically decreased the amount of high-cholesterol foods in his diet. It turned out he had replaced the high-fat cuts of beef with pre-breaded chicken breasts, and the breading was high in trans fat. (He later admitted that he was also eating more doughnuts, which, although cholesterol free, were rich in trans fat. Like the chicken breading, they too had an adverse effect on his cholesterol and also his waistline.)

Trans fats, unlike natural fats, have no known health benefits. Over thirty years ago, reports began to surface regarding their detrimental effects. In 1975 researchers in England suggested a possible reason for the higher rate of cardiovascular disease among the poor was that they often ate fish-and-chips fried in oil containing trans fats. In 1994 the Center for Science in the Public Interest petitioned the FDA to require disclosure of trans fat content. The FDA agreed to include trans fats on nutrition labeling in 2003, and this requirement took effect in January 2006.

The increased awareness and the food labeling have been good, but keep one caveat in mind: there is no "beneficial" recommended daily allowance for trans fat. In other words, the less you eat, the better. Studies show the adverse effects of trans fats (specifically, their role in heart disease), are seen when as few as 2 to 7 grams are eaten per day. This translates into just 20 to 60 calories!

And there is a second qualifier: the FDA allows food manufacturers to claim a product as "Zero Trans Fats" if the amount of trans fat *per serving* is less than 0.5 grams. So "zero" really isn't "zero," and if you, like many people, eat two, three, or even four servings as a single serving, then your trans fat intake will double, triple, or quadruple. One way to get around these issues is to look not only at the nutrition label, but also at the list of ingredients. If the term "partially hydrogenated" appears on the list of ingredients, then remember, that is the process that creates trans fats. Then, let the consumer beware.

Daily Prayer

Lord, I thank You for blessing us with natural foods. Your bountiful earth has produced all types of food that will preserve our health and not destroy it. I know the challenge facing me when I set out to reduce trans fats from my diet. Keep me steadfast and encouraged in this effort to improve the health of myself and my family.

HEALTH FACT OF THE DAY
DAY THIRTY-SEVEN

Studies confirm that trans fats promote inflammation. In women, greater intake of trans fat was associated with increased inflammatory markers such as tumor necrosis factor, interleukin-6, and C-reactive protein. Since the presence of inflammation is an independent risk factor for cardiovascular disease, heart failure, and diabetes, the inflammatory effects of trans fats may account in part for their harmful effects on cardiovascular health.

HIGH FRUCTOSE CORN SYRUP

A longing fulfilled is sweet to the soul.
—PROVERBS 13:19

IGH FRUCTOSE CORN syrup (HFCS) is a sweetener made from corn, not the plants we typically associate with "sweetness" like sugar cane and sugar beets, which give us table sugar (sucrose). It is made by milling corn into corn starch, then processing the corn starch into corn syrup, which is almost entirely composed of the sugar known as glucose. Enzymes are added to the corn syrup changing the glucose into fructose. The end result is a sweetener—HFCS 90—that is about 90 percent fructose, although there are other ratios as well (HFCS 55 and HFCS 42).

Since its introduction in the 1970s HFCS use has increased, completely replacing table sugar in many foods and beverages. From a business standpoint, HFCS has clear advantages over sugar. In the United States, corn is abundant and inexpensive compared with sugar, making HFCS much cheaper to use. Because it is a liquid, it is easier to transport than sugar, and this also affects pricing. Foods containing HFCS have a longer shelf life and less freezer burn than foods made with sugar. So these factors have made HFCS the ideal sweetener for food manufacturers. Their preference is reflected in our consumption of HFCS, which now exceeds that of table sugar. In 2005 the average American consumed about 28.4 kilograms of HFCS compared with 26.7 kilograms of sucrose sugar.[1]

But what's good for business is not always good for our health. From the start, there have been health concerns relating to HFCS, with animal studies showing a connection to liver damage and obesity. Food manufacturers have dismissed such studies and maintain the effects on the body from HFCS are essentially the same as those of table sugar. Animal studies aside, we cannot ignore the parallel trends between obesity and the consumption of soft drinks sweetened with HFCS.

Some countries, including Mexico and Canada, still use sucrose in their soft drinks, but in the United States, the major soda manufacturers use HFCS. Between 1970 and 1990, HFCS consumption increased by more than 1,000 percent, in large part because of the switch from sucrose to HFCS in soft drinks. Our consumption of soft drinks increased by 135 percent between 1977 and 2001, and soft drinks are now the largest source of added sugars in the American diet. During this same interval, the incidence and prevalence of obesity have skyrocketed.[2]

It might seem rational to conclude that the reason we're gaining weight is because of all the *calories* in soft drinks and not the sweetener per se. After all, too much sucrose will cause weight gain as will too much HFCS. Some maintain the increased consumption of *sugar* is the problem regardless of whether it is sucrose sugar or fructose sugar.

But it turns out to be a little more complicated than that. For the reasons already given, HFCS has decreased the manufacturing cost of soft drinks. When the profit margin is good, it pays to market heavily. Yes, consumption of soft drinks has increased, but one of the reasons we now drink so much is in part related to brilliant marketing and advertising. Good advertising will yield an increase in consumption. And let's face it; twenty or thirty years ago, grocery stores did not devote entire aisles to nothing other than soft drinks, and fast-food restaurants served eight-ounce—not forty-two-ounce—sodas.

So HFCS has affected our consumption, but recent studies are showing a clearer connection between its consumption and our health. A recent study presented at the 2007 Scientific Session of the American Diabetes Association involved human (not rodent) subjects.[3] In it, volunteers who were overweight or obese consumed drinks sweetened with either fructose or glucose. At the end of the study, the fructose group had a 212 percent increase in the level of triglycerides, while the glucose groups' triglycerides dropped by 30 percent. In addition, the LDL cholesterol and other "bad" fats—i.e., substances that accelerate atherosclerosis—were all significantly increased in the fructose group but remained unchanged in the glucose group.

While the final report is not yet available, the investigators concluded that their preliminary data strongly suggests a connection between HFCS and not only weight gain but also weight-related disease. They advised that people at risk for diabetes or cardiovascular disease limit their consumption of fructose-sweetened beverages.

Certainly more studies are sure to be conducted on the metabolic effects of HFCS. But even while we wait for more answers, we must always use wisdom. If weight and weight-related illnesses are real or potential problems, and if calorie restriction includes having to dramatically cut the consumption of "empty" calories that have no nutritional value, then it seems this would be reason enough to just eliminate high-calorie beverages from the menu altogether. To me, that's just common sense.

Daily Prayer

Lord, I pray that You guard me against discouragement as I make a commitment to better health. Keep me zealous in my pursuit to take care of my body, Your temple.

HEALTH FACT OF THE DAY
DAY THIRTY-EIGHT

Obesity is a major risk factor for osteoarthritis of the knee. A 2005 study found that for every pound of weight lost, there is a four-pound reduction in the load exerted on the knee with every step taken during daily activities.[4] This means that a one-mile walk after losing ten pounds reduces the compressive load to each knee by 48,000 pounds.

ARTIFICIAL SWEETENERS

The fear of the LORD *is pure, enduring forever. The ordinances of the* LORD *are sure and altogether righteous. They are more precious than gold, than much pure gold; they are sweeter than honey, than honey from the comb. By them is your servant warned; in keeping them there is great reward.*

—PSALM 19:9-11

FOR DECADES, ARTIFICIAL sweeteners have been a source of controversy in every arena—the scientific community, business, government, and in the general public.

The sweeteners of the 1970s were cyclamate and saccharin, which both came under fire after being linked to bladder cancer in rats. Cyclamate was banned, and saccharin was required to include a warning label that its use could pose a health hazard.

Saccharin is still available as Sweet'N Low, but the more popular artificial sweeteners (and the ones more commonly used in soft drinks) are the newer compounds: aspartame (NutraSweet and Equal), acesulfame-K (Sweet One and Sunett), and sucralose (Splenda). Neotame, which is eight thousand times sweeter than sugar, received FDA approval as a general purpose sweetener in 2002.[1]

Strictly speaking, stevia is not an artificial sweetener but a plant derivative. The many species of herbs and shrubs that fall into the stevia category are indigenous to South and Central America, and their extracts have been used for centuries by Native Americans.

In the 1970s Japan began cultivating stevia for use as a sweetener, motivated in part by the uncertainties regarding the safety of cyclamate and saccharin. And now, stevia has become so widely used in Japan that it accounts for 40 percent of their sweetener market.

But the stevia story in the United States has been more complicated. In 1991, the FDA called stevia an "unsafe food additive" and restricted its import. Animal studies had been inconsistent—some showed a cancer-causing potential; others did not. While this uncertainty stemmed from laboratory data, proponents of stevia argued that the best evidence for safety was found not in lab animals but in observing populations of people who have used stevia for generations with no obvious detrimental effects. The ban on stevia remained in place until after the passage of the Dietary Supplement Health and Education Act of 1994. This act limited the FDA's authority in regulating dietary supplements and allowed stevia's approval as a food supplement but not a food additive.[2]

That being said, the question remains as to whether or not we should use these products. Let me preface my opinion by saying that nobody's answer will please everyone. In other words, this decades-old controversy is not likely to end now. So here goes.

There are three reasons why I don't use artificial sweeteners. The first is simple: I don't like their taste. Though I have never tried stevia, I find the other sweeteners leave a "chemical" taste, which I don't enjoy.

Reason two relates to safety. Yes, I know the data is extensive and the verdict points toward harmlessness. But there is no way to conduct well-designed, long-term studies on *humans* that will absolutely confirm their safety, so I choose to err on the side of caution. I know exactly how sugar is metabolized by my body. I cannot say the same for these products.

Finally, their use has not curtailed the obesity epidemic. In fact, it seems the more sweeteners we use, the heavier we're getting. An interesting study done on rats at Purdue University found that rats fed yogurt sweetened with saccharin consumed more total calories and gained more weight than rats fed regular feed and yogurt sweetened with sugar. The researchers speculated that over time, artificial sweeteners conditioned the rat's bodies to stop associating a sweet taste with calories, and this disrupted their ability to accurately assess their caloric intake. While rat studies cannot be extrapolated to humans, we cannot dismiss the parallel trends of obesity prevalence and the use of artificial sweeteners.

Is it possible that artificial sweeteners are giving us a false sense of security? Maybe the woman using a zero calorie sweetener in her coffee instead of a 15-calorie teaspoon of sugar feels justified in choosing a colossal muffin made with chocolate chips over a slice of whole grain toast. What if calorie-laden sugar keeps us mindful of the need for discipline and moderation in our eating, while artificial sweeteners encourage us to cast off restraint? It's hard to say, but it's certainly food for thought.[*]

---

[*] This article first appeared in the July/August 2007 issue of *Today's Christian Woman* magazine.

Daily Prayer

Lord, You have blessed me in my going out and my coming in. Your mercy toward me is great, and You are an ever present help in times of trouble. You have sustained me against dangers and harm and have protected me against the plans of the enemy. I exalt You and praise You in the mighty name of Jesus.

HEALTH FACT OF THE DAY

DAY THIRTY-NINE

Alcoholic drinks made with artificial sweeteners result in a faster rate of alcohol absorption into the blood stream than drinks made with sugar-based mixers.

DAY **FORTY**

THE DASH DIET

You are the salt of the earth. But if the salt loses its saltiness, how can it be made salty again? It is no longer good for anything, except to be thrown out and trampled by men.

—MATTHEW 5:13

THE DASH DIET is an excellent eating plan, but it is not for weight loss—though people following it may shed a few pounds as an added benefit. "DASH" stands for Dietary Approaches to Stop Hypertension. It is the diet specifically recommended for people with or at risk for hypertension. The DASH trial was a large study conducted about a decade ago to examine the effects of various nutrients on blood pressure. The results of this trial were so significant that the DASH eating plan became a standard recommendation for treating hypertension, along with other lifestyle approaches like weight loss and exercise.

High blood pressure is a major risk factor for cardiovascular disease, the number one cause of death in the United States, and is extremely common, affecting about 30 percent of the population. About a third of people with hypertension are not aware of it (one of the reasons it's called "the silent disease"), and 65 percent of people who know they have it still have poor blood pressure control.[1]

The DASH investigators hypothesized that the nutrients found in a diet rich in fruits, vegetables, and low-fat dairy products would act together to lower blood pressure. Their results did, in fact, confirm this. Participants following the DASH diet had an eleven-point drop in their systolic blood pressure, compared with those on the control diet. The DASH approach not only lowered blood pressure but also had other "heart-healthy" effects including lowering the LDL cholesterol.

The DASH diet is high in magnesium, potassium, calcium, and fiber and limits the total fat, saturated fat, and cholesterol. Fruits and vegetables are rich sources of magnesium and potassium, while low-fat dairy products (as well as some vegetables) provide calcium. These three minerals help to lower the blood pressure; sodium elevates it. I find there is much confusion regarding dietary sodium, so let's clarify the role it plays in our health.

First let's clarify terms. Sodium is a mineral essential for life and found naturally in foods. Table salt is sodium combined with a second mineral, chloride. When we use the term "salt," we are usually referring to table salt, which is 40 percent sodium and 60 percent chloride. Dietary sodium also comes from other nonchloride sources such as sodium bicarbonate (baking soda), monosodium glutamate (MSG), and sodium nitrate (a food preservative). A teaspoon of table salt is about 6,000 mg in total, with approximately 2,400 mg of sodium.

Sodium is essential for life, but we really don't need to worry about whether we're getting enough. Most of us consume far too much. Population studies show that as the dietary sodium increases, there is a concomitant increase in the prevalence of hypertension and in the incremental rise of blood pressure with age. This is why in primitive societies that use neither table salt nor processed foods, a normal blood pressure remains the "norm," even in old age. But here in the United States, where our average daily intake is about 4,000 mg of sodium for every 2,000 calories, the vast majority of adults can expect to develop high blood pressure at some point during the remainder of their lifetimes.

U.S. government agencies advise limiting the sodium in our diets to 2,400 mg or less per day, the guideline used on food and nutrition labels. In reading the food label, however, don't be misled into thinking the 2,400 mg "daily value" is a recommended amount. For many—especially the elderly, African Americans, and people with hypertension or diabetes, who tend to be more sensitive to the effects of sodium, 2,400 mg per day is much too much.

The majority of dietary sodium in the typical Western diet comes from processed foods and restaurant foods. Some canned and processed foods contain in excess of 1,000 mg per eight-ounce serving, and the average restaurant meal has between one and two teaspoonfuls of salt. This is why it's entirely possible to eat too much salt without ever touching the salt-shaker.

The DASH diet has the proven benefit of lowering the blood pressure through increasing dietary magnesium, potassium, and calcium, and decreasing dietary sodium. Recent studies show that the diets of adults with hypertension not only fail to comply with the DASH recommendations, but also have deteriorated consistently since it was first introduced a decade ago. Sadly, the adherence rate is lowest among

African Americans, young people, and the obese—those who would stand to benefit the most.[2]

Details on the DASH eating plan are available through the National Institutes of Health (http://www.nhlbi.nih.gov). The way we eat greatly influences our blood pressure, and high blood pressure is a major risk factor for cardiovascular disease, still the number one cause of death in the United States. With or without hypertension and with or without obesity, the DASH approach is worth following.

Daily Prayer

Father, I marvel when I consider how intricately my body is designed. I acknowledge that each time my heart beats, it is because You are gracious and kind to me. Thank You for the gift of life, and help me to appreciate it as a blessing from You.

HEALTH FACT OF THE DAY
DAY FORTY

Along with its role in lowering blood pressure, magnesium may also protect against the formation of gallstones. Gallstone disease is common in the United States, and cholesterol stones are the most common form. Magnesium is lost during food processing, and the highly processed Western diet has contributed to the decline in magnesium intake in the United States. Dietary sources of magnesium include fish, whole grains, nuts, legumes, seeds, and green vegetables.

DAY FORTY-ONE

WEIGHT LOSS MEDICATIONS

For this very reason, make every effort to add to your faith goodness;
and to goodness, knowledge; and to knowledge, self-control; and to self-
control, perseverance; and to perseverance, godliness; and to godliness,
brotherly kindness; and to brotherly kindness, love. For if you possess
these qualities in increasing measure, they will keep you from being inef-
fective and unproductive in your knowledge of our Lord Jesus Christ.
But if anyone does not have them, he is nearsighted and blind, and has
forgotten that he has been cleansed from his past sins.

—2 PETER 1:5–9

WEIGHT LOSS MEDICATIONS have been around for years. Older drugs worked by suppressing the appetite or by speeding up the metabolism. Amphetamine was the prototype weight loss medication of the 1950s and 1960s. Use was limited because of adverse side effects, along with a significant risk of addiction. This potential for addiction served to stigmatize the pharmacological approach to weight loss for many years. In recent years, much research is being devoted to the development of new drugs. Some of these drugs have been approved for long-term use; others have not yet been approved in the United States; and still others have been withdrawn from the market because of safety concerns.

In 1992 reports of successful weight loss through use of a combination of two drugs, fenfluramine and phentermine, gained widespread attention. The "fen-phen" combination took the country by storm.[1] The demand for these drugs was so great that weight loss "clinics" began popping up all over the place. For a sizable fee, you could leave one of these establishments with a coveted fen-phen prescription, regardless of whether you needed it or not. Many "patients" who were prescribed fen-phen were *not* obese; some weren't even overweight. It was widely prescribed for cosmetic purposes in the absence of solid medical indications.

In 1996 the drug dexfenfluramine received approval for use as a weight loss medication.[2] Until this time, the Food and Drug Administration had not approved any medications for weight loss for twenty-three years.

188

Unlike fenfluramine, dexfenfluramine was authorized for continuous use up to a year. The drug was so popular that 3.3 million prescriptions were written from June 1996 to April 1997. In the spring of 1997, reports began to surface that people using fenfluramine and dexfenfluramine were developing abnormalities in their heart valves. Soon thereafter, the FDA withdrew both drugs from the market.[3]

Two prescription drugs were released subsequent to the withdrawal of fenfluramine and dexfenfluramine, which have FDA approval for long-term use. These are sibutramine and orlistat. Orlistat became available in an over-the-counter formula in February 2007.[4] A third drug, rimonabant, has been available in several countries in Europe and South America since 2006.[5] In 2007, however, the Advisory Committee of the FDA determined that more safety information was needed before the drug could be approved in the United States.[6]

Sibutramine works as an appetite suppressant. It, like some anti-depressant drugs, alters the balance of chemicals in the brain such as norepinephrine, serotonin, and dopamine. Studies have shown that patients taking sibutramine were able to lose 7 to 8 percent of their initial body weight over the course of a year, compared to a 1 to 2 percent loss in patients taking a placebo.[7]

Some of the side effects of sibutramine include headache, dry mouth, constipation, and insomnia. There have been reports of elevations in blood pressure and pulse rate; for this reason, people using sibutramine should have these monitored at regular intervals.

Orlistat works in an entirely different manner. It has no central nervous system effects and does not suppress the appetite; it works at the level of the intestine through preventing the absorption of dietary fat from the intestines into the bloodstream. Obviously, fat that never gets into your bloodstream cannot add inches to your waistline, but herein lies the mechanism for some of the more distressing side effects: oily stool, loose stool, flatulence, and (for some) a loss of bowel control. These effects are not universal, but they are fairly common. Some of my patients who have used orlistat are convinced it works purely through negative reinforcement—they tend to eat less fat just to avoid the potential for embarrassment.

There is also a concern that orlistat may impair the absorption of the four vitamins that require an oil-based medium to dissolve—vitamins A, D, E, and K. Because of this, patients are advised to take a multi-vitamin supplement containing these four vitamins. Patients who respond to prescription strength orlistat can expect to lose 8 to 10 percent of their initial body weight in six to twelve months.[8]

Neither sibutramine nor orlistat is approved for cosmetic weight reduction. These drugs should only be prescribed to patients who are obese or to patients who are overweight and have a weight-related medical condition. With the current high prevalence of obesity and its health consequences, much research is currently devoted to developing medications to curtail the problem. I anticipate we will see additional drugs available in the near future.

Daily Prayer

Eternal Father, You are omniscient with perfect wisdom. I know there is nothing created without Your sovereign knowledge, and You are Lord over every type of medical advance. I ask that You give me insight and discernment in making decisions pertaining to my health, including those decisions relating to prescription medications.

HEALTH FACT OF THE DAY
DAY FORTY-ONE

A recent study showed the symptoms of gastroesophageal reflux disease (GERD) rise progressively with increasing BMI, even among people with a normal body weight. Even moderate weight gain caused or worsened symptoms of GERD, while weight loss was associated with a decreased risk for symptoms.[9]

BARIATRIC SURGERY

This day I call heaven and earth as witnesses against you that I have set before you life and death, blessings and curses. Now choose life, so that you and your children may live.

—DEUTERONOMY 30:19

BARIATRIC SURGERY ("WEIGHT loss" surgery) has been around since the 1950s but has become more popular over the last decade as the prevalence of obesity has increased. The operation changes the anatomy of the stomach and intestinal tract, modifying either the stomach alone or the stomach and the small intestine combined.

More than one type of bariatric procedure is available. They can be broadly categorized into those that restrict the amount of food you can eat and those that decrease the number of calories absorbed. The restrictive procedures include gastric stapling, the vertical (sleeve) gastrectomy, and the adjustable gastric band. The latter is so appealing because the band is fully adjustable and the procedure can be done laparoscopically (through a small surgical incision in the abdomen).

The operation some consider to be the gold standard is called the Roux-en-Y gastric bypass. It both restricts the stomach's capacity and also prevents the absorption of calories by bypassing a portion of the small intestine.

The thought of surgery may seem dramatic at first, but depending on the patient, the body weight, and the presence or absence of weight-related medical conditions, it could prove to be a totally reasonable option.

Obviously the patient should be well informed about the procedure and know what to expect after the operation is over. Bariatric surgery will not get you "off the hook" in terms of following a healthy lifestyle. All patients must be motivated to implement good eating and exercise habits. Most health plans require documentation that medically supervised weight loss attempts have failed and a preoperative psychiatric assessment is in order. Depression is extremely common and would need to be treated prior to having any procedure.

Studies indicate the long-term success rate for bariatric surgery exceeds that for diet and exercise alone. Surgery is actually the treatment of choice for people with extreme obesity, defined as a body mass index (BMI) over 40, who have failed traditional approaches to weight loss (i.e., lifestyle modification and prescription medications).

The BMI is calculated using weight and the height. *Overweight* is defined as a BMI greater than 25; *obese* as a BMI greater than 30; and *extreme obesity* is any value over 40. It is estimated that about 5 percent of the total adult population has extreme obesity, but the percentage is higher in some subgroups. For instance, 16.5 percent of all African American women aged forty to fifty-nine have a BMI of 40 or more. Their prevalence of extreme obesity more than doubles that of white women (7 percent) and Mexican American women (7.8 percent) who are the same age.[1]

Another thing to consider in making a decision about bariatric surgery is whether there are medical conditions influenced by body weight like type 2 diabetes, sleep apnea, and hypertension. In these instances, surgery is appropriate with a BMI of 35 or more. Diabetes in particular responds well to bariatric surgery with many patients experiencing full remission of the disease.

If you have been in the valley of decision over bariatric surgery, are in the extreme obesity category, or suffer from medical conditions caused by body weight, make it a point to talk things over with your family and your primary care physician. Ask your doctor to refer you to a surgeon who can give you even more information about the surgery. This is not a decision to take lightly, and the Scriptures say that there is wisdom in a multitude of counselors. Seek God as you determine whether this procedure is right for you.*

Daily Prayer

> *Lord, I pray for clarity of thought in making decisions that pertain to my health. I ask that You remove anything that would prevent me from being objective or hinder my ability to do what is best for me. Please surround me with wise men and women who are able to provide me with sound advice and godly counsel.*

---

*This article first appeared in the July/August 2008 issue of *Today's Christian Woman* magazine.

HEALTH FACT OF THE DAY
DAY FORTY-TWO

In patients who have bariatric surgery, several psychosocial factors have been associated with a less than optimal outcome. These factors include disturbed eating habits (e.g., binge eating), substance abuse, low socioeconomic status, limited social support, and unrealistic expectations of surgery.

DAY **FORTY-THREE**

OBESITY AND DIABETES

"For I know the plans I have for you," declares the LORD,
"plans to prosper you and not to harm you, plans to give you
hope and a future."

—JEREMIAH 29:11

AS THE PREVALENCE of obesity and overweight has increased over the past few decades, there has been a parallel increase in the prevalence of type 2 diabetes. These two conditions are so tightly linked that the term *diabesity* was coined to emphasize the connection between the two. Before examining some of the issues relating to type 2 diabetes, let's clarify terminology.

Diabetes exists in two forms—type 1 diabetes and type 2 diabetes. Type 1 diabetes was previously called insulin-dependent diabetes or juvenile onset diabetes. This form is less common, constituting 5 to 10 percent of all cases of diabetes. In type 1 diabetes, the cells in the pancreas that make insulin are destroyed by an immune-mediated process. What triggers this process is not entirely clear, whether genetic, environmental, or an auto-immune disorder. It is usually diagnosed in children and youth, and there is no known way of preventing it. Type 1 diabetics always require insulin. They cannot be treated with oral medications. This form of diabetes is not connected to the obesity epidemic.

Type 2 diabetes constitutes 90 to 95 percent of all diabetes cases. In years past, it's been known as non–insulin dependent diabetes or adult onset diabetes. Both of these terms are misleading since many type 2 diabetics require insulin and not all cases are diagnosed in the adult years. Type 2 diabetes, unlike type 1, does not begin with insulin *deficiency* but rather insulin *resistance*. The cells of the body do not respond properly to the insulin produced by the pancreas (i.e., the body *resists* the insulin present in the bloodstream). To compensate, the pancreas of the type 2 diabetic will make more insulin. Over time, however, the pancreas loses its ability to produce insulin—it "burns out." At this point, the type 2 diabetic will require insulin, even though they may have been controlled with oral medications or lifestyle modification when the disease was initially diagnosed. Weight loss serves to reverse this insulin resistance, making the body more sensitive to it and preserving the function of the pancreas.

There are many risk factors for type 2 diabetes. Of course, obesity is a significant risk factor as is a sedentary lifestyle, but there are other risks as well. Age, family history, and race play a major role. African Americans, Hispanics, Native Americans, some Asian Americans, and Native Hawaiians are all at increased risk. Women who developed diabetes during pregnancy have a 20 to 50 percent chance of developing type 2 diabetes within five to ten years after delivery.

Over a million cases of diabetes are diagnosed each year. Today, 7 percent of the population has diabetes, which translates to 20.8 million people. Of this total, 6.2 million people remain undiagnosed. To make a serious matter even more somber, 54 million people currently have prediabetes and can be expected to progress to the full disease in the absence of lifestyle modification.[1]

Diabetes is a major risk factor for cardiovascular disease, the number one cause of death in the United States. In addition to heart disease, peripheral vascular disease, and stroke, there are other complications of diabetes, including kidney failure, hypertension, blindness, amputation, nerve damage, periodontal disease, depression, and difficulties during pregnancy.

It is an expensive disease. In 2007, the direct medical cost attributable to diabetes was $116 billion. The total annual economic cost, which includes medical expenditures along with indirect costs from employment losses, disability, and premature death, was $174 billion.[2]

Lifestyle modification with dietary changes, regular exercise, and weight loss can actually prevent diabetes from developing in people at risk. The same lifestyle changes will optimize the control of those already diagnosed with the disease and reduce the chance for complications.

Given that our bodies are the temple of the Holy Spirit, that this same Spirit equips us to make permanent changes for better health, and that Christians are called to be assets to our society instead of liabilities, it seems prudent that we would be eager to implement whatever change was required to optimize our health.

Daily Prayer

Lord, I pray You quicken in me a desire to live a lifestyle that will preserve, protect, and optimize my health. I understand that when I choose to live according to the flesh, even the economy stands to suffer with added health care costs. Teach me to be totally dependant upon Your Spirit, who will help me experience victory in my health.

HEALTH FACT OF THE DAY

DAY FORTY-THREE

Research demonstrates a link between insulin resistance, a key component of type 2 diabetes, and sleep apnea, independent of the role obesity plays in both conditions. In addition, there is accumulating evidence for an independent association between the metabolic syndrome and sleep apnea.

WEEKLY ASSESSMENT

My weight:	My BMI:	My waist size in inches:

I upheld my covenant by:

(Use a pencil and shade in the boxes starting from left to right to show how well you upheld your covenant this week.)

Less than 25%	25–49%	50–74%	75–99%	100%

VICTORIES: _____

_____

_____

_____

_____

_____

_____

PITFALLS: _____

_____

_____

_____

_____

_____

_____

Accepting the Weight Loss Process

DAY **FORTY-FOUR**

COPING WITH CHANGE

There is a time for everything, and a season for every activity under heaven.

—ECCLESIASTES 3:1

ONE OF THE most difficult things about losing weight is accepting that change is inevitable. There is comfort in the familiar, and this is why change is not easy. Just thinking about breaking old or even bad habits can generate anxiety.

Even when a change is implemented, the tendency to regress back to the old way of doing things never seems to go away. This is why New Year's resolutions are so often doomed to failure. Our initial enthusiasm for the positive change wanes with time, and the "bad habit" recurs before the end of January.

Several years ago, James Prochaska wrote an article in which he described how people go about changing an undesirable behavior.[1] He observed that when we try to break a harmful or addictive habit, we unconsciously proceed through five different phases. Each phase draws us closer to the point where we are totally successful in reaching our goal. Let's review these phases and try to identify where you are presently in terms of weight loss.

Precontemplative

The first phase of change is called the *precontemplative* stage. People in this stage have not yet acknowledged that they even have a problem. If they go through the motions of changing the behavior, it's usually to appease someone else and not because they are genuinely interested in changing. For example, an employer might threaten to fire an alcoholic employee unless he starts attending Alcoholics Anonymous meetings. The employee will go through the motions and attend A.A., not because he acknowledges a drinking problem, but because he fears losing his job.

Many overweight and obese people stay in this first stage out of igno- rance—they are simply unaware that their excess weight imposes a risk to their health. If you are reading this book, I'll assume that you've proceeded beyond the precontemplative stage and are, at the minimum, in the second phase of change.

Contemplative

The second phase of change is the *contemplative* stage. In this stage there is acknowledgment of a need for change, but no steps are taken to make it happen. This phase can last for years; some have spent their lifetimes contemplating a lifestyle change. A good example is the pack-a-day cigarette smoker who reads the Surgeon General's warning, agrees with it, admits that he should quit, and then proceeds to light up.

Preparation

The third phase is known as the *preparation* phase. The light has dawned, a decision is made, and the person begins to map out a strategy for reaching their goal. Plans for action are considered and choices made for implementation.

Action

Preparation is closely followed by the *action* phase. People in these two phases have taken steps, however small, toward changing their behavior. If you are reading this book because you sincerely want to lose weight or because you want to know how your spiritual life influences your physical condition, you probably belong in one of these two phases—you're either preparing for change or you are actively working at it.

Maintenance

The final stage of the cycle of change is *maintenance*. Once the change is implemented, our improved health requires that we maintain our new lifestyle for the long term. In my opinion, this is the most challenging of all five phases. The challenge is twofold; it involves an *internal* test and an *external* test.

The inner test is in resisting the tendency to return to old habits. The external test comes in dealing with the negative expectations of others. All eyes seem to be on the person in the maintenance phase. Many of those eyes are anticipating the weight to return.

The goal: termination

It's not uncommon—in fact, it's expected—for people to cycle through these phases of change over and over again. For example, the average cigarette smoker has tried to quit more than once. With each successful attempt, he proceeds through the five stages of change but falls back to one of the initial phases when he resumes the habit. Ideally, he'll eventually reach the point where he is completely freed from smoking. When that happens, he has reached the successful goal of termination. This sometimes, but not always, requires a person to cycle through the five phases several times.

Whatever phase you happen to find yourself in, the truth is that in order to lose weight and keep it off, something must change, and the change must be permanent. Hopefully, you have decided to make a change *before* receiving a diagnosis of a weight-related disease. The onset of these diseases can be delayed, or in some cases entirely prevented, if lifestyle changes are implemented early on.

Typically, it is not *one* change that is necessary for successful weight loss, but *three*:

- Our attitude about food
- The types and amounts of foods we eat
- Our commitment to physical activity

Assuming that because you are reading this book you have passed the precontemplation stage that denies any need for change, it will be helpful to highlight some things you may encounter during the next phases.

Overweight people in the second phase of change can become paralyzed from a lack of self-confidence. They don't deny that obesity is a problem, but their uncertainty in their ability to succeed prevents them from even trying. This is especially common in people who have weight cycled and find themselves back in phase two after repeated attempts to lose weight. Their fear of experiencing yet another failure will keep them from venturing beyond this second phase.

The third phase, preparation, is usually very practical. It's when we accomplish those things that get us ready to lose weight—menu planning, getting comfortable with new cooking techniques, and fitting exercise into our daily schedules. Most importantly, we prepare ourselves spiritually by acknowledging that the Lord we serve is more powerful than any force that might tempt us to neglect our health.

The action phase closely follows the preparation phase, as we have mentioned. The action phase of losing weight is an uplifting time. As we approach our weight loss goals, there is a satisfying sense of being in total control. This, along with the accompanying physical benefits of weight loss—increased level of energy, fewer aches and pains, and improved sleep—makes the action phase the most exhilarating.

The exhilaration is usually short lived because what follows is the fifth and most challenging phase of change—maintenance. Statistics show that long-term success in weight loss is dismally low with only 5 to 10 percent of people being able to keep the weight off for longer than five years.[2] Most go on to become "yo-yo dieters," who lose weight only to regain it again.

Why is the maintenance phase so challenging? Much of the failure is due to an inability to adapt to the new lifestyle required for maintaining a healthy weight and the fact that we simply cannot stop yearning for the harmful habits of the past.

Success in the maintenance phase, however, requires that we accept lifestyle changes as permanent: self-indulgence is replaced by self-denial; excess is replaced by moderation; sedentary is replaced by active. This is not as difficult to do if we choose to think on the positive rather than the negative. Rather than focusing on the things we *cannot* do or *cannot* eat, we must turn our attention to all the delicious foods available for us to eat that are nourishing to our bodies, as well as the long-term benefits of being physically active.

The Holy Spirit empowers us to achieve victory in each phase, even reaching the final step of "termination," where the cycling ends. This is where we will truly appreciate food as the blessing God intended it to be.

Daily Prayer

Father, I accept the inevitability of change. Help me to focus on the benefits that come in breaking bad habits, and grant me the strength to eliminate them from my life. Help me also to grow beyond the mistakes of the past that were detrimental to my health and to stay motivated to press on to a future of better choices.

HEALTH FACT OF THE DAY
DAY FORTY-FOUR

The risk for weight gain and type 2 diabetes is increased in women who have a high consumption of sugar-sweetened beverages.[3]

DAY **FORTY-FIVE**

THE INEVITABILITY OF HUNGER

Let them give thanks to the LORD for his unfailing love and his wonderful deeds for men, for he satisfies the thirsty and fills the hungry with good things.

—PSALM 107:8–9

W E HAVE BEEN fooled into thinking that it is possible to lose weight and keep it off without ever once experiencing hunger. Weight loss plans are promoted under the premise that you can eat what you want, never feel hungry, and still shed pounds effortlessly. This is simply not true. The sooner we reject this notion, the better. Yes, there are drugs available that are designed to suppress the appetite, but these drugs should not be used indefinitely. One way or another, we have to come to terms with hunger and learn to tolerate it if we expect success.

I have a patient whose maximum weight was 230 pounds. She now weighs 170 and has maintained that weight for several years. When people ask her what is the secret to her success, she tells them, "Good old hunger." She experimented with a variety of different diets and weight loss plans, but they all eventually failed. Success came only when she accepted the inevitability of hunger, learned to tolerate it, and took responsibility to control the impulse to eat with abandon when she felt even the mildest sensation of hunger. In addition, she paid close attention to bodily cues so that she *stopped eating* once real hunger subsided—a simple, effective approach to weight loss, grounded in the biblical principle of self-control.

Hunger is a blessing. It is a signal "wired" into us before we are born that is necessary for our survival. If a baby had no awareness of hunger and did not respond with distress to the sensation of hunger, his or her life would be in jeopardy. For that reason, we should praise God for giving us the capacity to feel hungry. In fact, I think it is appropriate to respond with joyful thanksgiving whenever we feel it, if for no other reason than to change our attitude about the weight loss process.

Most of us would miss out on this opportunity for praise because we hardly ever allow ourselves to experience hunger. I will often, as a teaching point, ask audiences to recollect the last time they felt unshakable, bona fide, "growling-in-the-stomach" type hunger. The response from a high percentage of the listeners is an eye-opening, convicting inability to recall. We have fallen into the pattern of eating in response to nonhunger cues: the sight, smell, and availability of food, and whether it is "mealtime" are what dictates when we eat and how much we eat. A premise worth heeding is this: if you never feel hungry, chances are very high that you are eating too much!

So, the first step is to refrain from eating unless there are legitimate hunger cues. But even once we feel those cues, we must learn to control how we respond to them. Keep in mind, weight loss occurs when there is a consistent negative caloric balance. This simply means the calories we eat must be, on average, less than the calories we metabolize ("burn up"), and this must be the case for an extended period of time. Once we reach our goal weight, then the calories we eat should match the ones we metabolize in order to remain at the goal and not regain. If, however, what we eat is consistently in excess to what we metabolize, the extra calories will not disappear but will be stored as fat, and we will gain weight.

We feel hunger when the food most recently eaten is metabolized because it is at that point that our body must tap into our reserves in order to provide us with the energy we need. While this is an extremely simplistic overview of the complex physiology of hunger, it suits our purposes. The most important point is that if we want our stored calories (i.e., our fat) to be metabolized (i.e., go away), and we realize that hunger is the signal that tells us our reserve (i.e., our fat) is in the process of being utilized, then hunger is what we *want* to feel—what we *need* to feel—in order to get rid of some excess fat and lose weight. I hope this serves to clarify why the notion of losing weight without ever feeling hungry, though an excellent marketing strategy, is not in keeping with basic physiology.

Along with learning to eat in response to legitimate hunger rather than nonhunger cues, it is imperative that we select the right foods. We know that our diets should be comprised of mostly unrefined plant-based foods like whole grains, vegetables, fruits, legumes, and nuts because they provide the nutrients we need for optimal health. But unrefined plant-based foods are also useful for losing weight and maintaining the weight loss. This is because they are high in fiber. The refining process takes away this advantage because it reduces (or eliminates) the fiber.

Our digestive system requires a longer period of time to process high-fiber, unrefined carbohydrates than it does low-fiber, refined carbohydrates. Because of this slower processing rate, the sensation of hunger is delayed. This explains why a whole-grain muffin, for instance, will keep you feeling satisfied for a longer period of time than a muffin made of refined flour, even if the calorie count is the same. This becomes especially important for people who have diabetes, "prediabetes," the metabolic syndrome, or any risk factor for the development of diabetes. High-fiber diets can help to guard against the development of diabetes, and they make the glucose easier to control in people with diabetes.

Hunger was given to us by God, who also gives us wisdom and self-control to manage it during the weight loss process. Advertisements for weight loss plans have made us believe that hunger is our enemy. They suggest we can eliminate this "foe" and still see the number on the scale come down. This is simply not true. It is impossible to have your cake, eat it too, and lose weight in the process! Don't fall for the lie; instead, rely on the power of the Holy Spirit, and take control of your flesh.

Daily Prayer

> *Lord, I appreciate the fearful and wonderful way You have made me. I am thankful for the God-given signal of hunger, and I ask that You help me to use it in an appropriate way to regulate my eating. I know through the Holy Spirit I have power to subject my flesh, and I, like Jesus, can endure through limited periods of hunger to accomplish a greater purpose.*

HEALTH FACT OF THE DAY
DAY FORTY-FIVE

A study conducted on twelve men with normal body weights showed that sleep deprivation influenced the levels of hunger-regulating hormones. The researchers concluded that it is possible that a chronic lack of sleep might contribute to overeating.[1]

DAY **FORTY-SIX**

DEALING WITH DOUBT

Now to him who is able to do immeasurably more than all we
ask or imagine, according to his power that is at work within us,
to him be glory in the church and in Christ Jesus throughout all
generations, for ever and ever! Amen.

—Ephesians 3:20–21

THE ELEVENTH CHAPTER of the Book of Hebrews opens with a profound truth: "Now faith is the substance of things hoped for, the evidence of things not seen" (v. 1, kjv). God is not someone we see with our natural eyes, but through faith, we have solid evidence of His existence. Believing in God requires faith, and believing in what God is able to do requires a double dose of faith—first to believe that He exists, and second to believe that He is able to work in the lives of His people.

Somewhere between the faith to believe in God and the faith required to believe that God is able we find a quagmire of doubt, which is where many are losing the weight loss battle. They believe that God exists, but they cannot be sure that He is able to help them in their personal struggles.

Anyone who has ever weight cycled knows that with each new attempt to lose weight, the measure of self-doubt increases. That doubt is fueled by past failures. Each pound and every ounce that returns serve to strengthen the uncertainty. In due time, the doubt is strong enough to thwart any fresh attempts at weight loss.

People in the weight loss industry know that doubt is a formidable force. To counteract its power, they tantalize potential customers with promises that are nothing short of being too good to be true. So we muster up the confidence to try one more plan, only because the before-and-after testimonial photographs are incredible motivators.

Doubt is an issue common to every person. The issue is not a question of *whether* we will feel doubt; it is a question of how to handle doubt *when* it comes. The Bible gives many examples of men and women who experienced doubt. When the Lord told Moses that He would provide meat for the Israelites to eat in the wilderness, Moses responded by saying:

Here I am among six hundred thousand men on foot, and you say, "I will give them meat to eat for a whole month!" Would they have enough if flocks and herds were slaughtered for them? Would they have enough if all the fish in the sea were caught for them?"

—Numbers 11:21–22

The apostle Thomas, whom many have dubbed *doubting* Thomas, wanted tangible proof of the resurrection of Christ before he would believe. (See John 20:25.) And John the Baptist sent his followers to ask Christ, "Are you the one who was to come, or should we expect someone else?" (Matt. 11:3). One of the more poignant passages from the Bible is the account of the man whose son was possessed by a mute spirit. This desperate father cried out to Christ, "I do believe; help me overcome my unbelief!" (Mark 9:24).

In all of these examples, doubt arises partly because these very ordinary people were facing a discouraging set of circumstances. God called Moses to lead the Israelites out of slavery, and the people witnessed the hand of God move miraculously on their behalf. Despite this blessing, they became discontent and turned their backs on God once they were delivered. Moses was burdened and discouraged by their constant complaining.

For Thomas, it seemed that all hope in the coming Messiah died with the crucifixion of Jesus. He had devoted three years to following Christ and learning of Him. His loyalty to Jesus was evident in his willingness to die for Him (John 11:16). But when his hope was challenged, Thomas became overwhelmed with doubt.

John the Baptist had preached in the wilderness of the coming of Christ and how vitally important it was for everyone to prepare themselves for the Messiah. But soon after baptizing Jesus and proclaiming to His followers, "Look, the Lamb of God, who takes away the sin of the world!" (John 1:29), he found himself alone and wrongfully imprisoned.

And finally, the father of the mute son had lived with his son's condition for all of the child's life. He had surely sought medical attention many times throughout the years, and he likely felt periods of hope after being prescribed a new form of treatment or a new medication. But the illness continued to plague his son, and every recurring seizure must have brought with it the sting of disappointment.

Disappointment or discouragement can cause feelings of doubt in the most mature believers. Certainly if John the Baptist, who was aware of the presence of Christ while he was yet in his mother's womb, could feel a twinge of doubt, then we should not be surprised when we feel it. For many who struggle with being overweight, the disappointment and discouragement that come with a failed diet plan or regained weight sets the stage for doubt.

What, then, is the best way to handle doubt? First, let's look at the wrong way. Doubt becomes a problem when it is not acknowledged for what it is. Many erroneously believe that feelings of doubt negate their faith. They have a tendency to suppress those feelings because they rationalize that acknowledging doubt is tantamount to accepting they have weak faith. What they fail to realize is that God is omniscient and discerns the heart. We cannot hide our emotions from Him. He knows the feelings we suppress as fully as He knows the ones we admit.

Doubt does not indicate an absence of faith. It only signifies that faith is being challenged. John the Baptist was a man of strong faith, but when he was imprisoned for speaking the truth, doubt surfaced. Rather than hide his doubt or ignore it, he took it to the only One who could alleviate it—Jesus Christ, who responded to his honesty not with a rebuke but with words of encouragement (Luke 7:22–23).

Instead of suppressing our doubt, we should take it to the Lord. The discouragement and disappointment of weight regain and weight cycling will lead to doubt. If you have been discouraged to the point of never wanting to address the issue of weight control again, then realize your doubt is nothing more than an emotion produced from feelings of inadequacy and fear of failure. Our faith, on the other hand, reflects our belief in God and our knowledge of His love toward us. We aren't governed by our emotions but by our faith.

If past failures have had a negative influence on your resolve, then model your response after the man with the mute son. First, accept the fact that the problem is too great for you to handle alone. If by your own power you were able to control your weight, then you wouldn't have a weight problem to contend with. The man with the mute son was certain that he was powerless to help his boy.

Second, believe that with God's help you can make permanent lifestyle changes to improve your health.

And finally, with sincere humility, ask the Lord to remove your doubt, and then take the step toward accomplishing this through earnest prayer.

The man with the mute son did not ignore his doubt. Instead, he brought it to the Lord with honesty and openness. Just like this desperate father, when we begin to lose hope, we ought to be quick to cry out, "Lord, help my unbelief."

Daily Prayer

Father, I ask that You encourage me today and help me to properly deal with issues of doubt. Help me to learn from past experiences and not be victimized by them. Let every failed attempt I've ever made serve as proof that I am weak but You are yet strong. Lord, be glorified in my weaknesses so that doubt cannot prevail.

HEALTH FACT OF THE DAY
DAY FORTY-SIX
To maintain weight loss, observational studies indicate that physical activity of moderate intensity (e.g., brisk walking) for approximately 80 minutes per day, or vigorous activity (e.g., jogging) for 35 minutes per day is protective against weight regain.[1]

FAD DIETS

The plans of the diligent lead to profit as surely as haste leads to poverty.

—PROVERBS 21:5

I F THERE IS one thing that will get us off track when it comes to accepting the weight loss process, it is the tendency to try fad diets. Our daily verse speaks of haste leading to poverty, but haste in the weight loss process also has negative consequences: disillusionment, disappointment, and discouragement.

One of the reasons why the weight loss industry is so lucrative is because we are willing to spend money on fad diets that promise short-term results, yet we are not as willing to make a lifelong commitment to healthy eating and regular exercise. There is a quality in human nature that desires "something for nothing." It's this tendency that makes fad diets so appealing—they promise a quick and easy solution to a complex and difficult problem.

There are literally hundreds of fad diets available. Some are based on a single food item where the dieter is allowed to eat the particular food in excess but limits everything else. Other fad diets are based on a specific nutrient like protein. Still others have no rhyme or reason and are based on things that aren't related to food at all. The following are examples of just a few of the more popular fad diets.

The grapefruit diet

The specific instructions for this diet vary depending on the source, but in general, the plan requires that a whole or half of a grapefruit be eaten before each meal. The dieter is also encouraged to drink lots of coffee or tea. This diet is based on the premise that grapefruit contains an enzyme that burns fat. In reality, no such enzyme has ever been discovered. Grapefruit is a good source of vitamin C and folic acid and should be part of any healthy diet, but like any other food, it shouldn't be eaten exclusively or in excess. If you happen to lose weight on this diet, then it is because grapefruit is a low-calorie, low-fat food—not because of any mystery enzyme.

Everyone who drinks coffee knows that caffeine has a diuretic effect—it causes excessive urination. So "success" with the grapefruit diet may simply result from dehydration—losing water weight, which will reaccumulate once you replenish your body's fluids. The combination of large amounts of citric acid and caffeine may also exacerbate gastroesophageal reflux disease (GERD) in those who are susceptible.

The cabbage soup diet

This diet appeals to people who want to lose weight fast. It claims that up to ten pounds can be shed in a one-week period of time without ever feeling hungry. That claim alone should generate suspicion, but those who want a "quick fix" often lose sight of what makes (or doesn't make) common sense. This is also a single-food diet. Instead of grapefruit, the dieter is allowed to eat unlimited quantities of cabbage soup. The plan also recommends caffeine-containing beverages, so once again, any drop in the scale is likely to represent water weight.

High-protein diets

These diets are based on the premise that carbohydrates make us hungry, and this leads to overeating. The proposed solution is to eliminate carbohydrates from the diet and substitute them with large quantities of protein and fat.

One obvious problem with this approach is that it will lack many of the vitamins and nutrients that are found exclusively in carbohydrate foods. These diets may also generate ketones in the body, and high ketones can cause headaches, nausea, fatigue, and dizziness. There is some evidence to suggest that high-protein diets may adversely affect the kidney function. People with kidney diseases should never try these diets.

FAD DIETS UNRELATED TO FOOD

1. *Blood type.* In recent years, I have had several patients ask me to check their blood type. This is not considered a "routine" laboratory test, and I wondered why there was such a new surge of interest. I later learned that one popular diet recommends that certain foods be eaten (or avoided) based on the person's blood type. The theory is that the different blood types evolved over time, so those

individuals with more primitive blood types are better equipped to handle primitive foods like meat. Individuals with blood types that evolved more recently are better equipped to handle sophisticated foods like vegetables.

The flaw in this theory is that those components in our food that supposedly react to our blood are either destroyed through the process of cooking, or they are destroyed by the digestive enzymes in our gastrointestinal tract. As a result, these food components never even enter the bloodstream to interact with our particular blood type.

2. *Deep breathing.* There's another weight loss plan that recommends deep-breathing exercises. This weight loss plan claims that the extra oxygen taken into your body will generate more energy for fat metabolism. However, this theory does not line up with basic physiology. In simple terms, whether you sigh, pant, or yawn, a calorie is still a calorie, and the extra calories are stored as fat. Oxygen will not eliminate the need to eat less food.

3. *Hormone imbalance.* Another popular diet postulates that obesity is the end result of a hormonal imbalance. It claims that eating certain foods will somehow correct this imbalance and facilitate weight loss. Would that the epidemic of obesity resulted from a few wayward glands! Unfortunately, the problem is not one of hormones; it's one of calories.

Weight loss occurs when the calories we consume are consistently less than the calories we utilize for an extended period of time. Don't get burned by fad diets. Accept the weight loss process, and make permanent lifestyle changes for better health.

Daily Prayer

Lord, I thank You for the fruit of the Spirit of patience, which equips me to resist those things that are hasty and embrace the tried and true. Please continue to give me wisdom and discernment in everything I do, especially those things pertaining to my health.

HEALTH FACT OF THE DAY
DAY FORTY-SEVEN

Marketdata Enterprises, Inc., estimates that the total U.S. weight loss market was worth $55.4 billion in 2006 and is expected to reach $68.7 billion by 2010.[1]

DO MEDICATIONS AND SURGERY REFLECT WEAK FAITH?

My son, preserve sound judgment and discernment, do not let them out of your sight; they will be life for you, an ornament to grace your neck. Then you will go on your way in safety, and your foot will not stumble; when you lie down, you will not be afraid; when you lie down, your sleep will be sweet.

—**PROVERBS 3:21–24**

ALTHOUGH WE HAVE already discussed both weight loss medication and bariatric surgery, I felt that it was important to revisit this topic because of the concerns Christians have about these weight loss methods. People who know that I am a Christian and know that I believe in the power of the Holy Spirit are curious to know whether I prescribe sibutramine and orlistat (the weight loss medications available in the United States at this writing), and whether I refer patients to surgeons. The idea of taking a pill or having an operation to lose weight seems to run counter to all the spiritual principles that I emphasize, especially the principle of self-control. The answer to both questions is yes—I *do* prescribe medications, and I *do* send patients for surgical evaluations, even Christian patients. Am I, then, a hypocrite? Is it possible to strike a balance between my faith and my practice?

I take the following stance when it comes to medications and operations. I firmly believe that it is possible to lose weight through implementing permanent lifestyle changes such as following a healthy, calorie-appropriate diet, and getting adequate exercise. I believe that the power necessary to implement these changes is available to the Christian through the indwelling Holy Spirit. But I cannot ignore the reality that the principles that I have outlined in this fifty-day journey require a level of spiritual maturity that cannot be attained overnight. Many of my patients and the men and women I counsel are "babes in Christ." They are actively working to grow in their faith, but maturation takes time. Spiritual growth is not like enrolling in college or graduate school where (ideally) the end is ultimately achieved and a degree or certificate is bestowed upon the student. To the contrary, spiritual growth is an active process that continues throughout our entire lifetime.

So, I am faced with a dilemma; do I do nothing other than wait for them to grow strong enough in their faith so that they can lose weight through the power of the Holy Spirit alone? Or do I provide them with assistance in the form of medications and operations *while* they mature in their faith? I have selected the second option for one reason—the consequences of weight-related diseases don't wait for spiritual growth. I would do my patients a disservice if I refused to provide them with therapy that has proven efficacy and instead insisted that they work just a little harder at growing spiritually. It would be wrong for me to suggest their only approach is to devote whatever time is necessary for spiritual growth while the complications of diseases such as type 2 diabetes, hypertension, sleep apnea, and arthritis wreak havoc on their bodies.

I believe in the power of the Holy Spirit, and I strongly recommend lifestyle modification (i.e., diet and exercise) as a sound approach to weight loss. But I must also use wisdom and consider each patient's circumstances. I would encourage you to seek God in prayer if you are contemplating weight loss medications or if you are seriously considering surgery. Neither decision should be taken lightly but only after you've sought godly counsel along with the advice of your health care provider. If your decision is to use medications or have an operation and you have found peace with it in prayer, then confidently proceed in that direction. Please don't think you've failed; don't get discouraged and—God forbid!—don't reckon that your faith is weak.

Daily Prayer

Lord, I acknowledge Your sovereignty and understand You are the One who gives man the ability to advance technology and medical science. I thank You, Father, that when my heart condemns me, You are greater than my heart and know all things. You grant peace and wisdom when I am faced with uncertainty, and You graciously guide me in making decisions for my life. Teach me to rest in Your truth rather than opinion.

HEALTH FACT OF THE DAY

DAY FORTY-EIGHT

Researchers compared the death rates after seven years in two groups of obese people: those who had gastric bypass surgery and those who did not. They found that long-term mortality was significantly reduced in the group who had surgery, particularly deaths from diabetes, heart disease, and cancer.[1]

ANYTHING WORTHWHILE TAKES TIME

The end of a matter is better than its beginning, and patience is better than pride.

—ECCLESIASTES 7:8

AFTER OUR FOURTH child was born, my husband and I decided we would buy a larger home. So when the baby was almost a year old, we moved into our present home, which, along with more space on the inside, also has more space on the outside. After we moved, I found that I couldn't shake a burning desire to start a garden in my new backyard.

Right now gardening happens to be one of my favorite pastimes, but at that time (being the city girl that I am), I had very little experience with it. As a child, I would help my mother plant flowers around the house each spring, and for a few years we even planted vegetables. But the kind of flower and vegetable beds I envisioned would require a level of skill and expertise that far exceeded my childhood experience. So I began reading books and watching television programs devoted to gardening, and I soon discovered that there was much more to it than simply buying a flat of marigolds, digging a hole in the ground to put them in, and hoping for rain.

In my studies I learned about annuals, perennials, and bulbs. I learned about hardiness, zones, and blooming times. I learned about fertilizers, weed killers, insecticides, and mulch. I learned about the various soil types—clay soil, sandy soil, and the coveted loam soil. I learned how to till the soil and how to amend the soil with organic matter like compost and peat moss. I even learned how to make my own compost with food waste from my kitchen that I would have ordinarily thrown in the garbage.

When I felt confident enough to actually plant something, I looked in a catalog from a mail-order nursery and came upon a picture of the flowerbed of my dreams. The bed contained nine different plants, each blooming at different times of the season, so I would enjoy flowers from the beginning of spring until late fall. Along with a detailed description of each plant, the catalog also provided a diagram of the size and shape of the flowerbed and mapped out the location where each plant should be placed.

I phoned in my order, and my husband and I took on the arduous task of clearing out a fifteen-by-five-foot plot of earth. We had a huge amount of sod to remove and an even more challenging task of preparing the soil. After much sweat and many sore muscles, we were finally ready for the arrival of my plants.

This was my first time ordering plants from a catalog, and I didn't know what to expect. I was quite surprised when the shoebox-sized package arrived. Having cleared such a large amount of ground and having prepared such a voluminous quantity of soil, the small box and its sparse contents of plants with delicate leaves and fragile stems planted in two-inch plastic containers was hardly what we imagined. Nearly half of the plants had no green at all—they were just clumps of brown, dry, gnarled roots inside sealed plastic bags.

Feeling disappointment well up inside, I went back to the catalog and noticed some fine print. Sure enough, it said that I shouldn't expect to enjoy the garden that was pictured for at least three seasons. The flowerbed of my dreams was to begin with a few tiny roots strategically placed in sixty square feet of earth. In spite of all the information I had gained from my studies, the first *real* lesson I learned in gardening was the lesson of *patience*.

Now, after I realized that the flowerbed I selected would require a minimum of three years to come even close to the catalog image, I had to make a simple choice: I could be patient, or I could be impatient. Patience would require me to painstakingly nurture and cultivate those delicate plants, season after season with few initial rewards. Impatience would cause me to throw up my hands at the prospect of waiting for long-term rather than instant rewards. The former approach would eventually lead to what I desired; the latter approach (though tempting) would ultimately result in a waste of my investment of time, labor, and money.

Keep in mind, I did not have a choice as to whether I would wait or not wait. My choice was limited to how I would *react* to the prospect of waiting. If I chose the right reaction—that of patience—then "the end of the matter" would truly be better than the beginning. A lush and colorful flowerbed would be much more aesthetic than a bed of weeds the ground would most certainly produce if left on its own as a result of my impatience. The three years were going to pass irrespective of my choice. What my choice *would* determine was the end result—a bed of flowers or a bed of weeds.

One of the most difficult things to accept when it comes to weight loss is the need for patience. As we discussed in the introduction, two pounds per week is a reasonable weight loss goal, but the person I'm regularly confronted with dismisses the slow and steady approach. The common scenario I experience is a woman in her late thirties or early forties who sees me in the office and asks me to assist her with losing weight. This typical patient might tell me that she did not have a weight problem as a child or even during her adolescent years, but since becoming an adult, she has steadily gained weight. Together we estimate that she's gained about five pounds per year and is now about sixty to seventy pounds heavier than she was on her wedding day.

And then she makes her plea. She "needs" to lose forty pounds in six weeks before leaving for a vacation in the Caribbean or attending her class reunion. Although she professes to want my help, she has already decided to try some fad diet or liquid diet she's read about, and is (cursorily) interested in my opinion. Or, she wants to know what I think about using "colon cleansers" or taking some pills she discovered in the health food store designed to boost her metabolism. She seems oblivious to the fact that it took well over a decade for her to accumulate the weight—she just wants it all gone in a month or two.

Patience is a virtue, and it is a characteristic of the Holy Spirit, being the fourth fruit of the Spirit found in Galatians 5. Our natural tendency is toward impatience, but as we learn to cultivate patience in our lives, it will help us to hold fast to the "end of the matter." As Solomon says in the verse for today, "The end of a matter is better than its beginning." When we become impatient (as we are prone to do), we set ourselves up for failure and disappointment. Learning to depend on the Holy Spirit to empower us to be patient involves not only a willingness to wait but also a willingness to endure whatever trials are destined to come our way during the waiting period.

Daily Prayer

Dear Father, help be to be patient today in all that I do. Guard my heart against haste and impulsiveness and replace it with the endurance that is Your will for me.

HEALTH FACT OF THE DAY
DAY FORTY-NINE

In a five-year study examining how often teens eat breakfast, an inverse relationship was found between BMI and breakfast frequency. As breakfast eating declined, the BMI increased; as breakfast eating increased, the BMI declined.[1]

DAY **FIFTY**

COMMIT TO THE PROCESS

I waited patiently for the LORD; he turned to me and heard
my cry. He lifted me out of the slimy pit, out of the mud and mire;
he set my feet on a rock and gave me a firm place to stand. He put
a new song in my mouth, a hymn of praise to our God. Many will see
and fear and put their trust in the LORD.

—PSALM 40:1–3

KING DAVID WROTE the Fortieth Psalm, and in it he uses a very descriptive metaphor to equate whatever difficulty he was experiencing to being stuck in a pit of slimy mud. His problem was a hindrance; it was distressing, and it kept him in bondage. While the passage does not specify the actual cause for his distress, it must have troubled him for a prolonged period of time, for he was required to *wait patiently.* The good news is that God responded to David's cry to deliver him from his unpleasant condition after he waited patiently for the Lord.

Why did the Lord require David to wait before he was delivered from the pit? And why are we required to wait in difficult circumstances, stuck in our own pits of life? Perhaps God has a different answer to those questions for each of His children. But one common element in the purpose of waiting is that there is a valuable lesson that can only be learned through a "pit" experience.

In those difficult pit experiences we are inclined to focus our attention on God as the source of our help. It is there that we receive from God the guidance and discipline that we would otherwise miss. God will make us stay in the mud until we have received all the "benefits" of the mud—He will keep us there as long as it takes to grow into His grace for our need. He will do all this because He loves us.

On day forty-four we discussed the process of change and how we cycle through the phases of change. I would equate this perpetual cycling to a pit experience. What, then, might be the lesson to be learned in this struggle? One seems clear: we can't do it on our own. Just when we think we will always maintain a proper perspective about food, just when we

223

think we have a handle on those obsessive thoughts about food, and just at the moment we feel we are stepping out of the pit of cycling and onto the firm foundation of the termination phase, something will predictably happen that causes us to slip right back into the slime. Then we find that after vowing to keep a tight control over candy, we eat a box of chocolates in one sitting, or after swearing to eat beef only in moderation, we indulge in an inch-thick twelve-ounce steak. The lusts of the flesh will invariably prevail when we rely on our own strength.

God will not pull us out of the pit if we are convinced we can get out on our own. But when we cry out to Him with a pure heart, when we come to Him broken and contrite, acknowledging our weaknesses and admitting that in and of ourselves we are powerless, then He will prove His faithfulness, pull us out of the weight cycling pit, and set us on solid ground. Deliverance comes by way of humble repentance and our acknowledgment of our total dependency on God. We must accept the reality that it is through the merciful forgiveness and the grace and power of God that we are able to overcome.

And so, through God's grace, you reach the termination phase. This was the goal, and it would be nice to conclude the process there, but we can't. The process continues with the *evidence* of the pit. No one comes out of a pit smelling like roses. Even though we rejoice that our feet are now planted on solid ground, we can't ignore the obvious: we're covered with mud and smell like slime. Specifically, our body is still overweight and our health has been compromised because of it.

By comparison, if we look at the experience of an alcoholic or drug addict at the point of exiting the cycle of change and reaching the termination stage, more often than not they find that their lives are in a state of total chaos. My husband has a very close friend who spent over twenty years in the pit of substance abuse. When he was in his mid-forties, he called upon the Lord and was born again. Then after his conversion, he spent another few years in the pit of addiction, trying over and over again to pull himself out by his own strength.

When he finally understood what it meant to be totally dependent upon Christ, the Lord released him from the bondage of addiction, he stopped cycling through the phases of change and reached the termination stage, and he has been drug free, alcohol free, and tobacco free ever since. But his life was a mess. The evidence of the pit was overwhelming—broken relationships, missed opportunities, and financial troubles. Facing his situation was especially painful because drugs and alcohol no longer clouded his perceptions.

The good news is that my husband's friend was able to get through this painful time because he was committed to the process. He allowed patience to govern him. He accepted the fact that the destruction in his life did not happen overnight and that the restoration process would involve some time as well.

When we finally put an end to cycling through the phases of change and rely on the power of the Holy Spirit to deliver us from the tendency to misuse food, as well as the tendency to yield to the flesh, it is a time to rejoice, but it can also be a time of great discouragement. The number on the scale reads exactly the same at the point of reaching termination as it did when you were still cycling through. Though you can rejoice that the spiritual bondage is gone, the pounds remain, at least initially. If there is no strong commitment to the process, feelings of discouragement with the "evidence" may be overwhelming. Without this commitment, all of the exuberance will give way to despair.

This is especially the case when the excess weight led to medical illness. The damage done to the body as a result of lifestyle-related diseases such as diabetes or hypertension may not be reversible. The arthritis that develops from constant inflammation and constant wear and tear on the weight-bearing joints may be permanent. The consequences of years, even decades, of exposure to a detrimental lifestyle won't just vanish into thin air once the eating and exercise habits improve.

But through it all, there is still reason to rejoice! Don't get discouraged—stay committed to the process. The termination phase means that what hindered you in the *spirit* realm has been conquered. The propensities to indulge the flesh, to yield to temptation, and to dismiss the call to lead a disciplined, self-controlled life are done away with at the termination phase. That gives reason to rejoice in the *spirit*, no matter what the condition of the *natural*.

If your health has been compromised by years spent with destructive habits, don't despair. The physical body is temporary; the spirit is eternal. Be encouraged by the words of Job, who said, "And after my skin has been destroyed, yet in my flesh I will see God; I myself will see him with my own eyes—I, and not another. How my heart yearns within me!" (Job 19:26–27).

Daily Prayer

Lord, I thank You for Your faithfulness and Your power to release me from perpetual weight cycling. Help me to stay committed to the process. Your very nature is patience, and You grant Your children the strength to endure. I also pray that You have mercy on me and heal my body from any damage caused by years of improper eating and inadequate exercise.

HEALTH FACT OF THE DAY

DAY FIFTY

It is estimated that each mile walked as part of a regular exercise program will extend your life by twenty-one minutes.

WEEKLY ASSESSMENT

My weight:	My BMI:	My waist size in inches:

I upheld my covenant by:

(Use a pencil and shade in the boxes starting from left to right to show how well you upheld your covenant this week.)

Less than 25%	25–49%	50–74%	75–99%	100%

VICTORIES: _____

_____

_____

_____

_____

_____

_____

PITFALLS: _____

_____

_____

_____

_____

_____

_____

AFTERWORD

Where there is no revelation, the people cast off restraint;
but blessed is he who keeps the law.

—PROVERBS 29:18

MORE THAN THE format has changed in this revision to the original *Spiritual Secrets to Weight Loss*. Some topics have been expanded upon; and some reduced in their content. It is my desire to honor the Lord's call by writing this issue. I hope I have effectively conveyed the magnitude of the problem and how solutions are not really hidden but definitely avoided.

I firmly believe the spiritual roots to the obesity epidemic have been ignored to our detriment. We have done "superficial weeding" with various weight loss plans and short-lived resolutions, plucking the dandelion at the base of the stem but doing little to eliminate the roots. I believe that this is why the problem has not gone away, and even more, it is affecting our children and our children's children.

But God has equipped us to get rid of the root. In the apostle Peter's second letter, he tells the believers:

> His divine power has given us everything we need for life and godliness through our knowledge of him who called us by his own glory and goodness. Through these he has given us his very great and precious promises, so that through them you may participate in the divine nature and escape the corruption in the world caused by evil desires.
>
> —2 Peter 1:3–4

Rather than use our power in Christ to "escape the corruption in the world caused by evil desires," we have done as the proverb indicates—we've "cast off restraint" when it comes to our eating and exercise habits. Now we are experiencing the consequences of excessive illness and premature death, not to mention the spiritual rewards we have forfeited by disregarding God's precepts.

When the Lord first showed me the spiritual nature of the problem, I felt a strong call to write it down and make it plain. That seed bore the fruit of the original *Spiritual Secrets to Weight Loss*. This revised version has been structured in a daily format that has truly been a renewal for you, most certainly for me. I feel an even more urgent persuasion from the Holy Spirit, the Encourager, to continue to press on in this area, though the message is sometimes cutting, often convicting, and always unpopular.

I pray that this work has made a difference in your life and has served to remove any tendency to cast off restraints and that it has instilled in you a stronger desire to seek God's face and abide by His law. When this happens, prepare yourself to receive the blessing of better health.

—Kara Davis, MD

NOTES

INTRODUCTION

1. BrainyQuote.com, "Hippocrates Quotes," http://www.
brainyquote.com/quotes/quotes/h/hippocrate153531.html
(accessed April 9, 2008).

2. American Diabetes Association, "Virtual Grocery
Store," http://vgs.diabetes.org/planningmeals/serving_sizes.
jsp (accessed May 1, 2008). Copyright © 2008 American
Diabetes Association. From http://vgs.diabeters.org. Modified
with permission from The American Diabetes Association.

3. M. L. Dansinger et al., "Comparison of the Atkins,
Ornish, Weight Watchers, and Zone Diets for Weight Loss
and Heart Disease Risk Reduction," *Journal of the American
Medical Association* 293 (2005): 43–53.

4. R. R. Wing and J. O. Hill, "Successful Weight Loss
Maintenance," *Annual Review–Nutrition* 21 (2001): 323–341.

5. P. L. Lutsey et al., "Dietary Intake and the Development of
the Metabolic Syndrome," *Circulation* 117 (January 22, 2008):
754–761.

WEEK ONE: KNOW GOD
DAY 1: STARTING OUT WITH GOD

1. C. L. Ogden et al., "Prevalence of Overweight and Obesity
in the United States, 1999–2004," *Journal of the American
Medical Association* 295 (2006): 1549–1555.

2. Kenneth F. Ferraro, "Firm Believers? Religion, Body
Weight and Well-Being," *Review of Religious Research* 39
(1998): 224–244.

DAY 2: JEHOVAH-RAPHE—THE GOD WHO HEALS YOU

1. A. Mokdad et al., "Actual Causes of Death in the United States, 2000," *Journal of the American Medical Association* 291 (March 10, 2004): 1238–1245.

2. "Actual Causes of Death in the United States, 2000—Correction," *Journal of the American Medical Association* 293 (2005): 298.

DAY 3: THE GOD OF LOVE

1. K. R. Fontaine et al., "Years of Life Lost Due to Obesity," *Journal of the American Medical Association* 289 (2003): 187–193.

2. D. Alley et al., "The Changing Relationship of Obesity and Disability, 1988–2004," *Journal of the American Medical Association* 298, no. 17 (2007): 2020–2027.

3. L. B. Yates et al., "Exceptional Longevity in Men," *Archive Internal Medicine* 168, no. 3 (2008): 284–290.

DAY 4: JEHOVAH JIREH—THE GOD WHO PROVIDES

1. Mayo Clinic, "Mental Health: Binge-Eating Disorder," http://www.mayoclinic.com/health/binge-eating-disorder/DS00608 (accessed April 4, 2008).

DAY 5: THE GOD OF POWER AND AUTHORITY

1. D. Bravata et al., "Using Pedometers to Increase Physical Activity and Improve Health," *Journal of the American Medical Association* 298, no. 19 (2007): 2296–2304.

DAY 6: THE GOD OF SECOND CHANCES

1. Diabetes Prevention Program Research Group, "Reduction in the Incidence of Type 2 Diabetes With Lifestyle Intervention or Metformin," *New England Journal of Medicine* 346 (2002): 393–403.

DAY 7: THE GOD OF WISDOM

1. D. Rucker et al., "Long Term Pharmacotherapy for Obesity and Overweight: Updated Meta-Analysis," *British Medical Journal* 335 (2007): 1194–1199.

WEEK TWO: LOVE YOURSELF
DAY 9: WHAT TRUE LOVE IS

1. S. Krishnan et al., "Glycemic Index, Glycemic Load, and Cereal Fiber Intake and Risk of Type 2 Diabetes in US Black Women," *Archives of Internal Medicine* 167, no. 21 (2007): 2304–2309.

DAY 10: OUR BODIES, HIS TEMPLE

1. S. C. Gonçalves et al., "Obstructive Sleep Apnea and Resistant Hypertension," *Chest* 132 (2007): 1858–1862.

DAY 11: MANAGING THE CLOCK AND MINIMIZING STRESS

1. KidsHealth.com, "Healthy Eating," http://www.kidshealth .org/parent/nutrition_fit/nutrition/habits.html (accessed April 4, 2008).

DAY 12: TWENTY-FIRST-CENTURY IDOLATRY

1. S. J. Olshansky et al., "A Potential Decline in Life Expectancy in the United States in the Twenty-First Century," *New England Journal of Medicine* 352 (2005): 1138–1145.

DAY 13: MADE TO MOVE

1. I. M. Lee et al., "Exercise Intensity and Longevity in Men. The Harvard Alumni Health Study," *Journal of the American Medical Association* 273 (1995): 1179–1184.

DAY 14: CELEBRATE WITH FOOD

1. B. D. Dickinson et al., "Reducing the Population Burden of Cardiovascular Disease by Reducing Sodium Intake," *Archives of Internal Medicine* 167, no. 14 (2007): 1460–1468.

WEEK THREE: MAINTAINING THE RIGHT ATTITUDE
DAY 15: STAYING FOCUSED

1. National Institute on Aging, "New NIH-Supported Study Characterizes Social Networks of Family, Friends Influencing Obesity," July 25, 2007, http://www.nia.nih.gov/NewsAndEvents/PressReleases/PR20070725obesity.htm (accessed April 4, 2008).

DAY 16: WHAT WOULD JESUS THINK?

1. KidsHealth.com, "Healthy Eating," http://www.kidshealth.org/parent/nutrition_fit/nutrition/habits.html (accessed April 4, 2008).

2. Victor C. Strasburger and Barbara J. Wilson, *Children, Adolescents, and the Media* (N.p.: Sage Publications, 2002), 241.

DAY 17: AMBASSADORS FOR CHRIST

1. J. J. Putnam and J. E. Allshouse, "Food Consumption, Prices and Expenditures, 1970–97," Washington, DC: Food and Rural Economics Division, Economic Research Service, USDA: 1999, Statistical Bulletin No. 965.

2. S. A. French et al., "National Trends in Soft Drink Consumption Among Children and Adolescents Age 6 to 17 Years: Prevalence, Amounts, and Sources, 1977/1978 to 1994/1998," *Journal of the American Dietetic Association* 103 (2003): 1326–1331.

DAY 18: THE MIRACLE OF SERVING OTHERS

1. A. H. Eliassen et al., "Adult Weight Change and Risk of Postmenopausal Breast Cancer," *Journal of the American Medical Association* 296 (2006): 193–201.

DAY 19: DON'T LET FOOD ADVERTISING THROW YOU OFF

1. AdAge.com, "The Advertising Century," http://adage.com/century/slogans.html (accessed June 23, 2008).

2. Food Commission, "Advertising to Children: UK the Worst in Europe," *Food* magazine (January/March 1997).

DAY 20: YOUR ATTITUDE IS SHOWING

1. Harvey Simon, *The No Sweat Exercise Plan* (Columbus, OH: McGraw-Hill, 2005), 20, 23.

DAY 21: THE JOY OF THE LORD

1. M. L. Fitzgibbon et al., "Obese People Who Seek Treatment Have Different Characteristics From Those Who Do Not Seek Treatment," *Health Psychology*, no. 12 (1993): 342–345.

2. B. T. Walsk et al., "Placebo Response in Studies of Major Depression: Variable, Substantial and Growing," *Journal of the American Medical Association* 287 (2002): 1840–1847.

3. M. A. Whooley, "Depression and Cardiovascular Disease," *Journal of the American Medical Association* 295 (2006): 2874–2881.

WEEK FOUR: LIVE IN GRACE
DAY 22: THE LETTER OF THE LAW

1. R. Estruch et al., "Effects of a Mediterranean-Style Diet on Cardiovascular Risk Factors," *Annals of Internal Medicine*, no. 145 (2006): 1–11.

DAY 23: THE GRACE TO FORGIVE

1. C. L. Ogden et al., "Prevalence of Overweight and Obesity in the United States, 1999–2004," *Journal of the American Medical Association* 295 (2006): 1549–1555.

2. F. X. Pi-Sunyer, "NHLBI Obesity Education Initiative Expert Panel on the Identification, Evaluation, and Treatment of Overweight and Obesity in Adults—the Evidence Report," *Obesity Research* 6, supplement 2 (1998): 51S–209S.

3. J. D. Sargent et al., "Obesity and Stature During Adolescence and Earnings in Young Adulthood: Analysis of a British Birth Cohort," *Archives of Pediatrics and Adolescent Medicine* 148 (1994): 681–687.

4. S. L. Gortmaker et al., "Social and Economic Consequences of Overweight in Adolescence and Young Adulthood," *International Journal of Eating Disorders* 329 (1993): 1008–1012.

5. P. Blumberg et al., "Medical Students' Attitudes Toward the Obese and the Morbidly Obese," *International Journal of Eating Disorders* 4 (1985): 169–175.

6. J. B. Bartholomew et al., "Effects of Acute Exercise on Mood and Well-Being in Patients With Major Depressive Disorder," *Medicine and Science in Sports and Exercise* 37, no. 12 (2005): 2032–2037.

DAY 25: LIBERTY AND OUR COMMITMENT TO OTHERS

1. Lutsey et al., "Dietary Intake and the Development of the Metabolic Syndrome," 754–761.

Day 27: Count the Cost

1. N. A. Christakis et al., "The Spread of Obesity in a Large Social Network Over 32 Years," *International Journal of Eating Disorders* 357 (2007): 370–379.

2. W. H. Dietz et al., "Do We Fatten our Children at the Television Set? Obesity and Television Viewing in Children and Adolescents," *Pediatrics* 75 (1985): 807–812.

Day 28: Leaving a Healthy Inheritance for the Next Generation

1. K. A. Coon et al., "Relationship Between Use of Television During Meals and Children's Food Consumption Patterns," *Pediatrics* 107, no. 1 (January 2001): e7.

2. B. A. Dennison, T. A. Erb, and P. L. Jenkins, "Television Viewing and Television in Bedroom Associated With Overweight Risk Among Low-Income Preschool Children," *Pediatrics* 109 (2002): 1028–1035.

3. Ibid.

4. L. M. Powell et al., "Exposure to Food Advertising on Television Among US Children," *Archives of Pediatric and Adolescent Medicine* 161, no. 16 (2007): 553–560.

5. Ibid.

6. Nielsen Media Research, "Nielsen Media Research Reports Television's Popularity Is Still Growing," http://www .nielsenmedia.com/nc/portal/site/Public/menuitem.55dc65b4 a7d5adff3f65936147a062a0/vgnextoid=4156527aacccd010Vgn VCM100000ac0a260aRCRD (accessed April 30, 2008).

7. David Walsh, National Institute on Media and the Family, "Turn Off the TV at Mealtime," http://www.mediafamily. org/mediawisecolumns/tvmeal_mw.shtml (accessed April 30, 2008).

8. C. Zoumas-Morse et al., "Children's Patterns of Macronutrient Intake and Associations With Restaurant and Home Eating," *Journal of the American Dietetic Association* 101, no. 8 (2001): 923–925.

9. D. Neumark-Sztainer et al., "Family Meals and Disordered Eating in Adolescents," *Archives of Pediatric and Adolescent Medicine* 162, no. 1 (2008): 17–22.

10. M. W. Gillman et al., "Family Dinner and Diet Quality Among Older Children and Adolescents," *Archives of Pediatric and Adolescent Medicine* 9 (2000): 235–240.

11. M. E. Eisenberg et al., "Correlations Between Family Meals and Psychosocial Well-Being Among Adolescents," *Archives of Pediatric and Adolescent Medicine* 158 (2004): 792–796.

12. Jacobson M. Center for Science in the Public Interest, "Liquid Candy: How Soft Drinks Are Harming Americans' Health," www.cspinet.org/sodapop/liquid_candy.htm (accessed April 30, 2008).

13. Ibid.

14. G. Block, "Foods Contributing to Energy Intake in the US," *Journal of Food Composition and Analysis* 17 (2004): 439–447.

15. J. James et al., "Preventing Childhood Obesity by Reducing Consumption of Carbonated Drinks: Cluster Randomized Controlled Trial," *British Medical Journal* 328 (2004): 1237–1241.

16. M. Nestle, "Soft Drink 'Pouring Rights': Marketing Empty Calories to Children," *Public Health Reports* 115, no. 4 (July/August 2000): 308–319.

17. S. A. French et al., "School Food Policies and Practices: A State-Wide Survey of Secondary School Principals," *Journal of the American Dietetic Association* 102, no. 12 (2002): 1785–1789.

18. Kent Steinriede, "Sponsorship Scorecard 1999," *Beverage Industry* 8 (1999): 8–10.

19. A. M. Wolf and G. A. Colditz, "Current Estimates of the Economic Cost of Obesity in the United States," *Obesity Research* 6 (1998): 97–106; as quoted in Eric Schlosser, *Fast Food Nation* (New York: HarperCollins, 2002), 53.

WEEK FIVE: PRACTICE SELF-CONTROL
DAY 29: A WALL OF PROTECTION

1. L. Jahns et al., "The Increasing Prevalence of Snacking Among US Children From 1977 to 1996," *Journal of Pediatrics* 138, no. 4 (2001): 493–498.

DAY 30: ACCOUNTABILITY

1. K. C. Eckstein et al., "Parents' Perceptions of Their Child's Weight and Health," *Pediatrics* 117, no. 3 (March 2006): 681–690.

DAY 31: GET A HOLD OF YOURSELF

1. J. Calle, "Obesity and Cancer," *BMJ* 335 (2007): 1107–1108.

DAY 33: UNCONTROLLED IMPULSES

1. Ogden et al., "Prevalence of Overweight," 1549–1555.

WEEK SIX: THE PRACTICAL AND THE SPIRITUAL
DAY 36: BODY FAT DISTRIBUTION

1. J. A. Simpson et al., "A Comparison of Adiposity Measures as Predictors of All-cause Mortality: the Melbourne Collaborative Cohort Study," *Obesity* 15 (2007): 994–1003.

2. S. M. Grundy et al., "Third Report of the Expert Panel on Detection, Evaluation, and Treatment of High Blood Cholesterol in Adults (Adult Treatment Panel III)." Executive summary. Bethesda, MD: National Institutes of Health; National Heart, Lung, and Blood Institute, 2001, NIH publication 01-3670.

3. Lutsey et al., "Dietary Intake and the Development of the Metabolic Syndrome," 754–761.

4. P. Bjorntorp, "Heart and Soul: Stress and the Metabolic Syndrome," *Scandinavian Cardiovascular Journal* 35 (2001): 172–177.

DAY 38: HIGH FRUCTOSE CORN SYRUP

1. United States Department of Agriculture Economic Research Service, http://www.ers.usda.gov/data/ foodconsumption/foodavailqueriable.aspx (accessed May 1, 2008).

2. S. J. Nielsen and B. M. Popkin, "Changes in Beverage Intake Between 1977 and 2001," *American Journal of Preventive Medicine* 27, no. 3 (2004): 205–210.

3. Emma Hitt, "Fructose but Not Glucose Consumption Linked to Atherogenic Lipid Profile," Medscape Medical News, http://www.medscape.com/viewarticle/559344 (accessed May 1, 2008).

4. S. P. Messier et al., "Weight Loss Reduces Knee-Joint Loads in Overweight and Obese Older Adults With Knee Osteoarthritis," *Arthritis and Rheumatism* 52, no. 7 (2005): 2026–2032.

DAY 39: ARTIFICIAL SWEETENERS

1. "Neotame: A Scientific Overview," http://www.neotame .com/pdf/neotame_science_brochure_US_New.pdf (accessed May 1, 2008).

2. U.S. Food and Drug Administration, "Dietary Supplement Health and Education Act of 1994, Public Law 103–417, 103rd Congress," http://www.fda.gov/opacom/laws/dshea .html (accessed May 1, 2008).

Day 40: The DASH Diet

1. C. L. Roumie et al., "Improving Blood Pressure Control Through Provider Education, Provider Alerts, and Patient Education," *Annals of Internal Medicine* 145, no. 3 (2006): 165–175.

2. P. B. Mellen et al., "Deteriorating Dietary Habits Among Adults With Hypertension," *Archives of Internal Medicine* 168, no. 3 (2008): 308–314.

Day 41: Weight Loss Medications

1. U.S. Food and Drug Administration Center for Drug Evaluation and Research, "Questions and Answers About Withdrawal of Fenfluramine (Pondimin) and Dexfenfluramine (Redux)," http://www.fda.gov/cder/news/ phen/fenphenqa2.htm (accessed April 28, 2008).

2. CenterWatch, "Drugs Approved by the FDA: Drug Name: Redux (Dexfenfluramine Hydrochloride)," http://www .centerwatch.com/patient/drugs/dru129.html (accessed April 28, 2008).

3. U.S. Food and Drug Administration, "FDA Announces Withdrawal of Fenfluramine and Dexfenfluramine," http:// www.fda.gov/cder/news/phen/fenphenpr81597.htm (accessed April 28, 2008).

4. U.S. Food and Drug Administration Center for Drug Evaluation and Research, http://www.fda.gov/CDER/drug/ infopage/orlistat_otc/index.htm (accessed April 28, 2008).

5. Medscape Medical News, Y. Waknine, "International Approvals: Accomplia and Abraxane," http://www.medscape .com/viewarticle/537382 (accessed April 28, 2008).

6. Medscape Medical News, S. Wood, "Unanimous 'No' to Rimonabant: Safety Not Demonstrated, FDA Advisory Panel Says," http://www.medscape.com/viewarticle/558224 (accessed April 28, 2008).

7. M. E. J. Lean et al., "Sibutramine: A Review of Clinical Efficacy," *International Journal of Obesity* 21, no. 1 (1997): S30–S36.

8. L. Sjöström et al., "Randomised Placebo-Controlled Trial of Orlistat for Weight Loss and Prevention of Weight Regain in Obese Patients," *The Lancet* 352, no. 9123 (1998): 167–172.

9. B. C. Jacobson et al., "Body-Mass Index and Symptoms of Gastroesophageal Reflux in Women," *New England Journal of Medicine* 354 (2006): 2340–2348.

DAY 42: BARIATRIC SURGERY

1. Ogden, "Prevalence of Overweight," 1549–1555.

DAY 43: OBESITY AND DIABETES

1. American Diabetes Association, "All About Diabetes," http://www.diabetes.org/about-diabetes.jsp (accessed May 1, 2008).

2. Ibid.

WEEK SEVEN: ACCEPTING THE WEIGHT LOSS PROCESS
DAY 44: COPING WITH CHANGE

1. J. O. Prochaska et al., "In Search of How People Change: Applications to Addictive Behaviors," *American Psychology* 47 (1992): 1102–1114.

2. R. W. Jeffery et al., "Long-Term Maintenance of Weight Loss: Current Status," *Health Psychology* 19, no. 1 (2000): 5–16.

3. M. B. Schulze et al., "Sugar-Sweetened Beverages, Weight Gain, and Incidence of Type 2 Diabetes in Young and Middle-Aged Women," *Journal of the American Medical Association* 292 (2004): 927–934.

DAY 45: THE INEVITABILITY OF HUNGER

1. K. Spiegel et al., "Brief Communication: Sleep Curtailment in Healthy Young Men Is Associated With Decreased Leptin Levels, Elevated Ghrelin Levels, and Increased Hunger and Appetite," *Annals of Internal Medicine* 141 (2004): 846–850.

DAY 46: DEALING WITH DOUBT

1. D. A. Schoeller et al., "How Much Physical Activity is needed to Minimize Weight Gain in Previously Obese Women?" *American Journal of Clinical Nutrition* 66 (1997): 551–556.

DAY 47: FAD DIETS

1. PR Web, "U.S. Weight Loss Market to Reach $58 Billion in 2007," http://www.prwebdirect.com/releases/2007/4/prweb520127.php (accessed May 1, 2008).

DAY 48: DO MEDICATIONS AND SURGERY REFLECT WEAK FAITH?

1. T. D. Adams et al., "Long-Term Mortality After Gastric Bypass Surgery," *New England Journal of Medicine* 357, no. 8 (2007): 753–761.

DAY 49: ANYTHING WORTHWHILE TAKES TIME

1. M. T. Timlin et al., "Breakfast Eating and Weight Change in a 5-Year Prospective Analysis of Adolescents: Project EAT (Eating Among Teens)," *Pediatrics* 121, no. 3 (2008): 638–645.

FREE NEWSLETTERS
TO HELP EMPOWER YOUR LIFE

Why subscribe today?

☐ **DELIVERED DIRECTLY TO YOU.** All you have to do is open your inbox and read.

☐ **EXCLUSIVE CONTENT.** We cover the news overlooked by the mainstream press.

☐ **STAY CURRENT.** Find the latest court rulings, revivals, and cultural trends.

☐ **UPDATE OTHERS.** Easy to forward to friends and family with the click of your mouse.

CHOOSE THE E-NEWSLETTER THAT INTERESTS YOU MOST:

- Christian news
- Daily devotionals
- Spiritual empowerment
- And much, much more

SIGN UP AT: **http://freenewsletters.charismamag.com**

8178

5'9"